Biography Today

*Profiles
of People
of Interest
to Young
Readers*

Volume 14
Issue 3
September 2005

Cherie D. Abbey
Managing Editor

Kevin Hillstrom
Editor

*615 Griswold Street
Detroit, Michigan 48226*

Cherie D. Abbey, *Managing Editor*
Kevin Hillstrom, *Editor*
Jeff Hill and Laurie Hillstrom, *Sketch Writers*
Allison A. Beckett, Mary Butler, and Linda Strand, *Research Staff*

* * *

Peter E. Ruffner, *Publisher*
Frederick G. Ruffner, Jr., *Chairman*
Matthew P. Barbour, *Senior Vice President*
Kay Gill, *Vice President — Directories*

* * *

Elizabeth Barbour, *Research and Permissions Coordinator*
David P. Bianco, *Marketing Director*
Leif A. Gruenberg, *Development Manager*
Kevin Hayes, *Operations Manager*
Barry Puckett, *Librarian*
Cherry Stockdale, *Permissions Assistant*

Shirley Amore, Don Brown, John L. Chetcuti, Kevin Glover,
Martha Johns, and Kirk Kauffman, *Administrative Staff*

Copyright © 2005 Omnigraphics, Inc.
ISSN 1058-2347 • ISBN 0-7808-0689-1

The information in this publication was compiled from the sources cited and from other sources considered reliable. While every possible effort has been made to ensure reliability, the publisher will not assume liability for damages caused by inaccuracies in the data, and makes no warranty, express or implied, on the accuracy of the information contained herein.

This book is printed on acid-free paper meeting the ANSI Z39.48 Standard. The infinity symbol that appears above indicates that the paper in this book meets that standard.

Printed in the United States

Contents

Preface

Biography Today is a magazine designed and written for the young reader —
ages 9 and above — and covers individuals that librarians and teachers tell
us that young people want to know about most: entertainers, athletes, writers, illustrators, cartoonists, and political leaders.

The Plan of the Work

The publication was especially created to appeal to young readers in a format
they can enjoy reading and readily understand. Each issue contains approximately 10 sketches arranged alphabetically. Each entry provides at least one
picture of the individual profiled, and bold-faced rubrics lead the reader to information on birth, youth, early memories, education, first jobs, marriage and
family, career highlights, memorable experiences, hobbies, and honors and
awards. Each of the entries ends with a list of easily accessible sources designed
to lead the student to further reading on the individual and a current address.
Retrospective entries are also included, written to provide a perspective on the
individual's entire career.

Biographies are prepared by Omnigraphics editors after extensive research,
utilizing the most current materials available. Those sources that are generally available to students appear in the list of further reading at the end of
the sketch.

Indexes

Cumulative indexes are an important component of *Biography Today*. Each
issue of the *Biography Today* General Series includes a Cumulative Names
Index, which comprises all individuals profiled in *Biography Today* since the series began in 1992. In addition, we compile three other indexes: the Cumulative
General Index, Places of Birth Index, and Birthday Index. See our web site,
www.biographytoday.com, for these three indexes, along with the Names
Index. All *Biography Today* indexes are cumulative, including all individuals
profiled in both the General Series and the Subject Series.

Our Advisors

This series was reviewed by an Advisory Board comprised of librarians, children's literature specialists, and reading instructors to ensure that the concept of this publication — to provide a readable and accessible biographical magazine for young readers — was on target. They evaluated the title as it developed, and their suggestions have proved invaluable. Any errors, however, are ours alone. We'd like to list the Advisory Board members, and to thank them for their efforts.

Gail Beaver
Adjunct Lecturer
University of Michigan
Ann Arbor, MI

Cindy Cares
Youth Services Librarian
Southfield Public Library
Southfield, MI

Carol A. Doll
School of Information Science and Policy
University of Albany, SUNY
Albany, NY

Kathleen Hayes-Parvin
Language Arts Teacher
Birney Middle School
Southfield, MI

Karen Imarisio
Assistant Head of Adult Services
Bloomfield Twp. Public Library
Bloomfield Hills, MI

Rosemary Orlando
Director
St. Clair Shores Public Library
St. Clair Shores, MI

Our Advisory Board stressed to us that we should not shy away from controversial or unconventional people in our profiles, and we have tried to follow their advice. The Advisory Board also mentioned that the sketches might be useful in reluctant reader and adult literacy programs, and we would value any comments librarians might have about the suitability of our magazine for those purposes.

Your Comments Are Welcome

Our goal is to be accurate and up-to-date, to give young readers information they can learn from and enjoy. Now we want to know what you think. Take a look at this issue of *Biography Today*, on approval. Write or call me with your comments. We want to provide an excellent source of biographical information for young people. Let us know how you think we're doing.

Cherie Abbey
Managing Editor, *Biography Today*
Omnigraphics, Inc.
615 Griswold Street
Detroit, MI 48226

editor@biographytoday.com
www.biographytoday.com

Congratulations!

Congratulations to the following individuals and libraries, who are receiving a free copy of *Biography Today*, Vol. 14, No. 3 for suggesting people who appear in this issue:

Rachel Q. Davis, Thomas Memorial Library, Cape Elizabeth, MD

Mary Louise Helwig-Rodriguez, Little Falls Public Library, Little Falls, NJ

Kimberly Lentz, North Rowan High School Media Center, Spencer, NC

Nicole Nava, Austin, TX

Kristen Bell 1980-

American Actress
Star of the Critically Acclaimed TV Series
"Veronica Mars"

BIRTH

Kristen Anne Bell was born on July 18, 1980, in Huntington Woods, Michigan, a quiet suburb of Detroit. She is the only child of Tom Bell, a television news director, and Lori Bell, a registered nurse. Her parents divorced before she turned two. Kristen lived with her mother in Huntington Woods and eventually gained a stepfather, radio account manager Ray

Avedian, and two stepsisters. Her father remarried and eventually moved to Phoenix, Arizona, but maintained a close relationship with Kristen.

YOUTH

Growing up, Kristen gained a reputation as an active, strong-willed girl. "She was a pill; she was a handful," her mother acknowledged. "She was always active, always knew her mind. She was the no-fear girl." At the age of four, Kristen announced that she no longer liked her first name. Instead, she declared that she wanted to be named after her favorite television characters, the Smurfs. "I cleverly swayed her away from the cartoon characters and towards her middle name, Anne, which is also her grandmother's name," her mother remembered. To this day, many of Kristen's old friends call her Annie.

> ———— " ————
>
> *"She was a pill; she was a handful," her mother acknowledged. "She was always active, always knew her mind. She was the no-fear girl."*
>
> ———— " ————

Bell began modeling for catalogs as a girl and signed with an agent by the time she entered her teens. Her first acting experience came at the age of 12 at the Stagecrafters community theater in Royal Oak, Michigan. She became so nervous before her first audition that she broke down in tears. Luckily, her mother was able to convince her to go through with the audition. "My mom said to me, 'Go in there and do what you said you were going to do and recite your Shel Silverstein poem or whatever in front of those 13 people,'" Bell remembered. "'You're so nervous; we never have to come here again. But you owe it to yourself.'"

Bell won a role in the Stagecrafters production of "Raggedy Ann and Andy." "It was a complex dual role actually," she joked. "I played a banana in the first act and I played a tree in the second act. I know you're thinking—how could I balance two characters like that? But somehow I did it." Despite her rough audition, Bell came to love appearing on stage. "The ability to pretend and the sense of family it provided became addicting," she related. "In youth theater, you get a whole bunch of kids together and allow them to think and create and receive recognition for their work. It gives them a voice and an outlet to explore their own creativity, which makes for a better adult, regardless of whether or not a child chooses acting as their profession."

When Bell was 17, her best friend was killed in a car accident. She has called the tragedy "both the best and worst thing that has ever happened to me. I think I'm a happier person because of it, as weird as that is because once you learn not to take people for granted, you live a l̶ pier life." She also used this experience of early loss in creating her ⸝⸝⸝ ⸝⸝ sion character Veronica Mars.

EDUCATION

Bell attended the Burton International School, a multicultural school for gifted students in kindergarten through eighth grade. She went on to attend Shrine High School, a Catholic school in Royal Oak. Before graduating in 1998, she impressed audiences with her singing and acting ability as Dorothy in Shrine High's production of *The Wizard of Oz*.

Bell then moved to New York City to attend New York University's prestigious Tisch School of the Arts. She left the program in 2001, a few credits shy of earning her bachelor's degree, in order to accept a role in a Broadway play. Bell expressed some bitterness about the school's decision not to award her degree. "The weird thing is they gave me credit for bringing people coffee [as an intern], but they wouldn't give me credit for being on a Broadway stage every night," she explained.

CAREER HIGHLIGHTS

Appearing on Broadway

Bell became a fixture on the New York theater scene both during and after her time at NYU. Her first major role was as Becky Thatcher in the musical version of *Tom Sawyer* that played in New York in 2001. Bell also starred opposite the well-known film actors Liam Neeson and Laura Linney in the 2002 Broadway production of Arthur Miller's *The Crucible*.

Bell first gained widespread attention, however, for her portrayal of the squeaky-clean girl-next-door Mary Lane in the musical adaptation of *Reefer Madness* in New York. The play was based on a low-budget 1936 propaganda film about the dangers of marijuana. The original intent of the film was to scare people away from drugs. But it exaggerated the effects of marijuana use so dramatically (claiming that a few puffs could drive people insane and cause them to commit murder, for example) that it seemed campy, and it became a cult classic in the 1960s. "They were essentially B-movie actors who thought they were going to make a movie that would change the views of America; it was meant to be serious," Bell said of the original film. "It wasn't until they saw [the finished product] that they realized it was looking like a spoof."

Bell's character in the play, Mary Lane, falls in love with Jimmy, played by Christian Campbell. But Jimmy tries marijuana and is soon seduced into the world of drugs, which causes him to experience wild hallucinations and eventually go insane. Ultimately, though, the stage revival of *Reefer Madness* was intended to be a raucous musical comedy. In a review for *USA Today*, Elysa Gardner called it "a delirious romp, which at its best reaches highs of intoxicating goofiness."

In 2002 Bell moved to Hollywood. The creators of *Reefer Madness* planned to create a film version of the successful musical, and they wanted her to reprise her role as Mary Lane. In fact, they convinced her to move to California and offered her a place to stay for the first few months. The movie version of *Reefer Madness* appeared on Showtime in 2005. "Ultimately, the film's a bauble, unsubtle but full of such theatrical pep that one feels something real for these ridiculous characters in their exaggerated plight," Robert Lloyd wrote in a review for the *Los Angeles Times*. "Such are the intoxicating powers of musical theater—beware!"

Living in Hollywood

Living in Hollywood, Bell tried to make a career in television and film. She won a role on the 2002 season premiere of "The Shield," a gritty police drama broadcast on FX. She played a gang member's girlfriend who is raped and tattooed on the face. Although she auditioned for a number of TV series and movies over the next year, it took her a while to get another part. "It was very grounding to be that close to so many things and not get them," she recalled.

Finally, Bell received the starring role in the 2003 Lifetime original movie *Gracie's Choice.* As the teenaged daughter of a drug-addicted welfare mother, she had to decide whether to escape to a new life with her boyfriend or take responsibility for her younger siblings. *Detroit Free Press* reviewer Mike Duffy described the TV movie as "a powerful story of one working-class teen taking control of life despite the family-bruising trauma of her neglectful mother's drug abuse."

In 2004 Bell received her first major role in a theatrical release. In *Spartan,* a film by the respected independent director David Mamet, she played the wild daughter of the U.S. president. When she disappears with one of her college professors, she becomes the subject of an intensive search. Investigators eventually discover that she has been abducted into a white slavery ring. Some critics found *Spartan* difficult to follow, and the movie received mixed reviews.

The cast of "Veronica Mars."

Starring in "Veronica Mars"

In 2004 Bell heard about a new television series, "Veronica Mars," that would appear on the UPN network. The series was created by Rob Thomas, a former writer for "Dawson's Creek" and the author of the acclaimed young adult novels *Rats Saw God* and *Slave Day*. Bell soon auditioned for the lead role. She loved the script and the character, and she was thrilled to get the part over 100 other actresses who auditioned. "Kristen was actually the second actress who auditioned. And it was over for me. She was the person I wanted," said series creator Rob Thomas. "Veronica out-savvies people.

13

Kristen has to play really, really smarter than you. Hiring this NYU-trained Broadway actress is so much different from casting another pretty LA girl."

"Veronica Mars" is set in the wealthy oceanside community of Neptune, California. The main character, 17-year-old Veronica, is a student at Neptune High School. At one time she had been part of the popular crowd, along with her wealthy and beautiful best friend, Lilly Kane. But then Lilly was murdered, and Veronica's father, Sheriff Keith Mars (played by Enrico Colantoni), took charge of the investigation. Keith felt that the evidence pointed to Lilly's powerful and mysterious father, Jake Kane. When he was cleared of responsibility for the crime, Keith lost his job as sheriff. The scandal convinced Veronica's troubled mother to leave the family and turned Veronica into an outcast at school. Her father starts a private investigation business, and Veronica spends her evenings working as an apprentice detective to help him. She sneaks around Neptune with a camera, trying to uncover the town's dirty secrets and solve her friend's murder case.

——— " ———

"I think every character I've played, I've been able to draw on something in my life. I'm a fighter. I'm a little bit of a firecracker like Veronica is. And her strength appeals to me."

——— " ———

Bell drew upon her own experience of a friend's death to create the character of Veronica. "When you have a loss at such a young age, you become bitter and jaded and your whole perspective changes," she noted. "Veronica wouldn't be who she is without it." She identified with the character in other ways, as well. "I think every character I've played, I've been able to draw on something in my life," she stated. "I'm a fighter. I'm a little bit of a firecracker like Veronica is. And her strength appeals to me." Bell considers herself lucky to be part of a new and different kind of TV series — one that combines teen drama and murder mystery. "It's like nothing else out there," she said. "Rob Thomas has created so many twists, once you start watching you won't be able to stop. Yet he's been able to completely base it in a realistic setting. It's about a normal girl. She's not a super girl, she's just trying to live life."

"Veronica Mars" received acclaim from TV critics as soon as the pilot episode aired in fall 2004. "It's one of the freshest and most original new series of the year," Mike Duffy wrote in the *Detroit Free Press*. "Series creator Rob Thomas has written a really smart, witty pop noir with a twist of postmodern Nancy Drew in the form of 17-year-old detective Veronica

Veronica (Bell) and her friend Wallace Fennel, played by Percy Daggs III.

Mars. Kristen Bell's performance is funny, intelligent, and emotionally affecting, the sort of breakout performance that can make her a star." Critics reserved a great deal of praise for Bell's performance as the title character. A *Variety* reviewer, for example, called her "as charismatic as she is tough and intelligent, giving a multilayered performance that touches on simple 17-year-old insecurity and convincingly incorporates deeper issues concerning family, love, and disappointment."

Despite the critical acclaim, however, "Veronica Mars" failed to attract a large audience and consistently ranked near the bottom of the weekly TV ratings. The three million people who do watch "Veronica Mars" tend to be deeply dedicated to the show, discussing the plot twists in Internet chat rooms and sending e-mails to UPN begging for it to be renewed. Bell says that the show resonates with teenagers and their parents. "We've been doing these mall tours where we [the cast] go to a city and have thousands of people line up," she noted. "I have girls and guys alike come up to me and say that, You know, I started watching your show, and sort of the way Veronica handles things has given me strength to come out of my shell or out of my depression or whatever their problems were." Similarly, mothers approach Bell and tell her that watching "Veronica Mars" with their teens has helped open up a dialogue about important issues. Despite lackluster ratings, the UPN network decided to renew the show for a second season.

Enjoying Her Work

Bell is often told that she looks young for her age. "I'm carded for R-rated movies," she admitted. "And I get talked down to a lot. When I try to rent a car or buy an airplane ticket or other stuff adults do, I get, 'Okaaaay, honey.' I remember when I was 18, getting crayons in a restaurant." Although her youthful appearance helps in her role as a high school student, she looks forward to expanding her range of characters. "I like playing teenagers, but it'll be nice when I can start playing girls in their 20s — without their parents around," she said.

Bell thoroughly enjoys her work as an actress, and she claims that would be the case even if she were not famous. "I'm not involved in the business of becoming famous," she stated. "And that's the advice I give to younger aspiring actors. Work on stage and do the little roles. In the end it's not important to be seen. It's important to do." Although she sometimes spends more than 15 hours per day on the set of "Veronica Mars," she still feels fortunate to be able to make a living doing what she loves. "I'm proud of being able to do what I do. I'm really lucky to be able to have been involved in some amazing projects with some amazing people," she noted. "I'm in a very, very good place that hundreds of thousands of actresses wish they were in. Although my schedule is grueling, I have to realize how badly I wanted it."

HOME AND FAMILY

Bell lives in Los Angeles with her boyfriend, Kevin Mann, who is a freelance writer, independent movie producer, and high school swim coach. They share their home with two dogs that they rescued from the pound.

HOBBIES AND OTHER INTERESTS

Bell is a big fan of the Detroit Red Wings and the Detroit Pistons. She celebrated when the Pistons won the 2004 NBA title by defeating the Los Angeles Lakers. "I represented when the Pistons won," she related. "I wore my 'Bad Boys' T-shirts and got some dirty looks in LA."

SELECTED CREDITS

Television

Gracie's Choice, 2003 (TV movie)
"Veronica Mars," 2004- (TV series)
Reefer Madness, 2005 (TV movie)

Film

Spartan, 2004

Stage

Tom Sawyer, 2001
Reefer Madness, 2001
The Crucible, 2002
A Little Night Music, 2004

FURTHER READING

Periodicals

Bergen (NJ) County Record, Dec. 14, 2004, p.F9
Daily Variety, Aug. 30, 2004, p.A21
Detroit Free Press, Aug. 1, 2004; Dec. 23, 2004
Detroit News, Sep. 22, 2004, p.D1
Entertainment Weekly, Oct. 29, 2004, p.59; Dec. 10, 2004, p.36
Los Angeles Times, Mar. 20, 2005, p.E27; Apr. 16, 2005, p.E1
New York Times, Jan. 12, 2004, p.E8; Nov. 7, 2004, p.ST4
USA Today, Apr. 27, 2001, p.E13; Oct. 8, 2001, p.D5; Mar. 12, 2004, p.E6;
     Sep. 22, 2004, p.D4
Variety, Sep. 20-26, 2004, p.70; Feb. 7-13, 2005, p.74
WWD, Oct. 11, 2004, p.24

Online Articles

http://entertainment.iwon.com
     (TV Guide Insider, "Is Veronica Mars a Pothead?" Apr. 15, 2005)

ADDRESS

Kristen Bell
UPN Television
11800 Wilshire Blvd.
Los Angeles, CA 90025

WORLD WIDE WEB SITES

http://www.tomsnet.net/kristenbell.html
http://www.upn.com/shows/veronica_mars_tmpl
http://www.upn.com/shows/veronica_mars/

Sergey Brin 1973-
Larry Page 1973-

Inventors of the Google Search Engine and Founders of Google Inc.

BIRTH

Sergey Brin was born on August 21, 1973, in Moscow, the capital of the former Soviet Union (now Russia). His family moved to the United States when he was six years old and settled in College Park, Maryland. His father, Michael Brin, is a professor of mathematics at the University of Maryland. His mother, Eugenia Brin, works as a specialist for the National Aeronautics and Space Administration (NASA).

Lawrence E. Page was born on March 26, 1973 in East Lansing, Michigan. His father, Carl Page, was a pioneer in the field of computer science who served as a professor at Michigan State University. His mother, Gloria Page, was a database consultant who also taught computer programming at the university. Larry has one brother, Carl Jr., who is nine years his senior.

YOUTH

Sergey Brin and his family left Russia because they faced anti-Semitism. They often endured taunts about their Jewish religion when they walked through the streets of Moscow. "I was worried that my children would face the same discrimination if we stayed there," Michael Brin noted. "Sometimes the love for one's country is not mutual." They made a new life for themselves in the United States, where Sergey grew up loving math and science.

Meanwhile, Larry Page inherited an early interest in computers from his parents and older brother. "I never got pushed into it," he recalled. "I just really liked computers." The Page family had a computer at home as early as 1979. "I turned in the first word-processing assignment in elementary school," Larry remembered. "No one even knew what a dot-matrix printer was." By the time he was 18, he had constructed a working inkjet printer out of Lego building blocks.

EDUCATION

Teaming Up

Brin attended high school in College Park, where he was a star of the chess club and math team. In fact, the school yearbook compared him to the brilliant physicist Albert Einstein. After graduating from high school in 1990, Brin went on to earn a bachelor of science (BS) degree—with a double major in mathematics and computer science—from the University of Maryland in 1993. He pursued graduate studies at Stanford University in California, earning a master of science (MS) degree in 1995. He remained as a candidate for his doctorate (PhD) at Stanford, where he met Larry Page.

Page graduated from East Lansing High School in 1991 and then enrolled in the College of Engineering at the University of Michigan. During his undergraduate years, he served as president of Michigan's branch of the national engineering honor society, Eta Kappa Nu. After receiving his bachelor of science degree in engineering in 1995, he decided to pursue graduate studies at Stanford. Page initially felt intimidated by the intense academic environment he found in Stanford's computer science department. "At first, it was pretty scary," he acknowledged. "I kept complaining to my friends that I was going to get sent home on the bus."

Brin and Page met shortly after Page joined Stanford's PhD program in 1995. At first, each student found the other "obnoxious," and they argued about every topic they discussed. But then they discovered a common interest in finding new ways to locate information on the rapidly growing World Wide Web. "I was working on data mining, the idea of taking large amounts of data, analyzing it for patterns, and trying to extract relationships that are useful," Brin recalled. "When Larry joined, he started dabbling with the Web and started gathering large amounts of data. That data intrigued me, and I wanted to run various experiments on it."

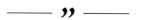

> "I was working on data mining, the idea of taking large amounts of data, analyzing it for patterns, and trying to extract relationships that are useful," Brin recalled. "When Larry joined, he started dabbling with the Web and started gathering large amounts of data. That data intrigued me, and I wanted to run various experiments on it."

Inventing a New Kind of Search Engine

For two years—from the beginning of 1996 to the end of 1997—Brin and Page worked together on a research project they hoped would help people make sense of the vast amount of information available on the Web. They developed a new type of Internet search technology that they called PageRank. This program used a set of complex mathematical algorithms to rank Web sites in order of importance, based on the number of links they received from other sites. "There are millions of variables, but we manage to do a lot of math, very fast, and in the end we rank pages in a way that's very close to how you would do it intuitively," Brin explained.

The two PhD candidates then incorporated their PageRank system into a revolutionary new search engine. They called this program BackRub, for its ability to analyze the "back links" pointing to a given Web site. At that time, most search engines were compiled by "spiders," automated devices that crawled across the Web and created a database of terms appearing on Web sites. When users searched for a specific term, the search engines returned a list of sites on which the term appeared. The approach taken by Brin and Page expanded upon traditional search engines by indexing not only terms, but also the popularity of a given Web site, based on the number of links it received from other sites.

BackRub consistently returned more relevant results than the leading search engines, and it quickly grew in popularity among Stanford students and faculty. "We didn't even intend to build a search engine originally," Page noted. "We were just interested in the Web and interested in data mining. And then we ended up with search technology that we realized was really good. And we built the search engine. Then we told our friends about it and our professors. Pretty soon, about 10,000 people a day were using it."

In the early years of development, Brin and Page attempted to sell their search technology to several large Internet companies, but they received little interest. Although some of these companies found BackRub impressive, they were not interested in upgrading their search capabilities at that time. Instead, they were busy exploring new Web applications, like chat and instant messaging. Brin and Page, however, believed that searching was a vital—and neglected—usage of the Web. "Search is important," Brin stated. "It's important for people to be able to find information quickly, easily, accurately, and objectively." Thinking that they had discovered a great opportunity, the students decided to start their own search engine business. They both left Stanford in 1998, before completing their doctoral degrees.

CAREER HIGHLIGHTS

Founding Google Inc.

Brin and Page called their fledgling business Google. They based the name on the mathematical term "googol," which means 10 to the power of 100 (10^{100}). According to Brin, this enormous number represented the ambitious mission of their company: "to organize the world's information, making it universally accessible and useful." While they were still students at Stanford, the two men used credit cards (their own and their parents') to buy enough computer disks to store a terabyte (a million megabytes) of information. Then they built their own computer housings in Page's dorm room, which became Google's first data center.

In the spring of 1998, Brin and Page showed their business plan to Andreas ("Andy") Bechtolsheim, a co-founder of Sun Microsystems. "We met him very early one morning on the porch of a Stanford faculty member's home in Palo Alto," Brin remembered. "We gave him a quick demo. He had to run off somewhere, so he said, 'Instead of us discussing all the details, why

Brin and Page in the server room at Google.

don't I just write you a check?' It was made out to Google Inc. and was for $100,000." Unfortunately, "Google Inc." did not officially exist yet, so Brin and Page could not cash the check. Over the next few weeks, they rushed to complete the paperwork needed to incorporate their business. Finally, Google Inc. was born, with Page as its chief executive officer and Brin as its president.

Once Google gained the support of a high-profile computer-industry executive like Bechtolsheim, Brin and Page had little trouble finding other investors. By September 1998 they had raised nearly $1 million—enough to fund Google's first year of operations. They moved out of Page's dorm room, opened up an office in a friend's garage, and worked hard to perfect and expand their search engine. When they unveiled the final version of the program in 1999, it became a tremendous hit with Web users. In fact, even without advertising, Google's user base grew by a remarkable 20 percent each month. "Search is the number-one application on the Web," Page explained. "And it's easy for people to try out different search engines so they can compare. They notice differences and tell their friends. Friends tell friends. And that's how we grow."

Google's popularity attracted interest from several major venture capital firms, which are companies that invest in unproven business ventures, in hopes that the businesses will experience rapid growth and provide a good return on the investment. Brin and Page collected $25 million in venture capital from two computer-industry investment firms. This large investment brought a great deal of attention to the small, unproven company, and instantly raised the profiles of its young founders.

Around this time, the Google search engine started to attract a great deal of media attention. Both industry journals and mainstream periodicals com-

"We didn't even intend to build a search engine originally," Page noted. "We were just interested in the Web and interested in data mining. And then we ended up with search technology that we realized was really good. And we built the search engine. Then we told our friends about it and our professors. Pretty soon, about 10,000 people a day were using it."

mented on Google's unique approach to ranking Web sites based on their popularity, which consistently delivered search results of superior quality and relevance. "Just as you trust the links on a really good site to get you to other good pages, Google crawls the Web scooping up hyperlinks and uses them to figure out how important a page is by who is pointing at it," Margot Williams wrote in the *Washington Post.* "Google interprets connections between Web sites as votes," Chris Taylor added in *Time.* "The most linked-to sites win the Google usefulness ballot and rise to the top of search results. More weight is given to 'voters' with millions of links themselves, such as Amazon or AOL." The *Wall Street Journal* praised Google for providing "a beacon in a sea of confusion" on the Web.

Growing with the Web

One of the challenges facing Brin and Page involved keeping up with the growth of the World Wide Web, which was expanding by more than 1.5 million pages every day. From the beginning, Google had to develop new software and increase its number of computers in order to keep pace. Some analysts compared Google's mission with finding a needle in an enormous haystack that grew larger every day. But Brin and Page refused to be intimidated by the exponential growth of the Web. In fact, Brin argued that the Google search engine would actually provide more accurate results over time because there would be more links for it to analyze. "That's our competitive advantage — we get smarter, not worse, as the Web gets bigger," he stated.

By mid-2000 Google had become the first search engine to index over a billion Web pages, making it the biggest in the world. Google also enjoyed an exceptional rate of customer satisfaction, with 97 percent of users reporting that they found the information they were looking for most or all of the time. These achievements helped Google earn a coveted Webby Award from the International Academy of Digital Arts and Sciences. In June 2000 Brin and Page announced the first in a series of lucrative partnerships with major Internet services: Google became the default search engine to complement Yahoo!'s directories.

Google's growth continued in 2001. By June of that year, the Google search engine handled over 100 million queries per day. Half of these searches were done using Google's Web site, and the other half were executed from the Web sites of various partners through licensing agreements. By the end of 2001, Google indexed 3 billion Web documents. Google Inc. also earned a profit that year — a feat that many Internet start-up companies never accomplish, and a particularly impressive achievement in the aftermath of the collapse of numerous Internet businesses in 2000. The success of Google attracted the attention of several large firms in the computer industry, but Brin and Page turned down all offers from prospective buyers. "We're growing at a good rate, we have been successful at attracting good [employees], and we are increasing our traffic tremendously," Brin said. "We believe we are going to dominate the market — and if you believe that, it's hard for anyone to pay you enough to justify selling."

In August 2001 Brin and Page decided to bring in an experienced manager to help them run their rapidly growing enterprise. They hired Eric E.

Schmidt, the former chief executive officer (CEO) of software maker Novell, to be Google Inc.'s new CEO. Page became president of products, while Brin became president of technology. "Larry focuses a little more on the operations side — computers and things like that," Brin explained. "I focus on research and marketing." One magazine described Page as "Google's clean-cut geek in chief, the brilliant engineer and mathematician who oversees the writing of the complex algorithms and computer programs behind the search engine," and called Brin "the company's earnest and impassioned visionary."

A massive sign outside the NASDAQ stock exchange welcomes Google after the company went public.

Going Public

Following the management reorganization, Google Inc. continued to grow. By the beginning of 2003, an amazing four out of every five searches conducted on the Web used Google, either directly from the Google home page or through another site that licensed its technology. The company stood far above virtually every other online business in terms of financial health, earning more than $100 million in profits on revenues of just under $1 billion.

In fact, Google had become so pervasive that the name of the search engine became a verb. For instance, people talked about "Googling" prospective dates and employers in order to obtain inside information. The search engine also helped people conduct academic research, locate long-lost relatives, recall old song lyrics, and simplify their lives in any number of ways. Google thus became "not only the place people go when looking for obscure factoids, but a pop-culture phenomenon," as Catharine P. Taylor wrote in *Brandweek*.

Google's remarkable success led many observers to speculate about when the company would "go public," or sell shares of ownership on the stock market for the first time. But Brin and Page resisted the idea of making

Charting Google's Growth

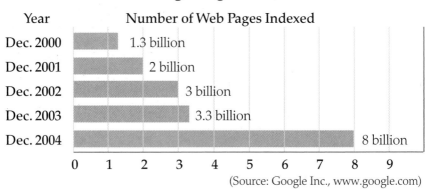

Year	Number of Web Pages Indexed
Dec. 2000	1.3 billion
Dec. 2001	2 billion
Dec. 2002	3 billion
Dec. 2003	3.3 billion
Dec. 2004	8 billion

(Source: Google Inc., www.google.com)

Share of U.S. Search Engine Market

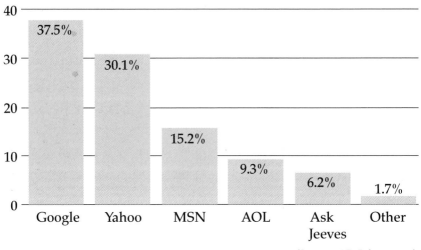

Google	37.5%
Yahoo	30.1%
MSN	15.2%
AOL	9.3%
Ask Jeeves	6.2%
Other	1.7%

(Source: AP, July 7, 2005)

Google Inc. a publicly held company. They enjoyed having complete control over operations, rather than having to explain their decisions to stockholders. They also appreciated the fact that small, privately owned companies are not required to report their financial results to the outside world. Over time, however, the founders realized that Google had reached a point in its growth where it made sense to go public. The venture capitalists who had funded the company's early operations were eager to cash out their investments. In addition, since Google Inc. had accumulated more than 500 employees, it would soon be required to report financial results like a public company.

Brin and Page soon decided to prepare the company for an initial public offering (IPO). An IPO marks the first time that a corporation offers shares of stock for sale to investors on the public stock exchange. Many corporations stage an IPO, or "go public," as they grow in order to get money to pay for further expansion. Investors who purchase stock become part-owners of the company. They gain or lose money based on the company's financial performance.

When Brin and Page finally decided to take Google public, their company was so successful that they were able to dictate the terms of the IPO. They announced that the stock sale would be conducted on August 19, 2004, using the little-known Dutch auction process. Although this process was supposed to help stabilize the price of the stock, many investors found it confusing. Some analysts criticized Brin and Page during the IPO process, calling their demands for control "arrogant" and the stock price they suggested "exorbitant." But Brin and Page felt that their arrangements for the IPO were necessary in order to maintain Google's culture and long-term focus.

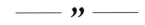

"Larry focuses a little more on the operations side — computers and things like that," Brin explained. "I focus on research and marketing."

On the day that the highly anticipated stock sale took place, shares started selling at $85 each and ended above $100. These results gave Google Inc. a valuation of $27 billion, which was not only the highest among Internet companies, but also higher than many industrial giants, like General Motors. Experts estimated that Brin and Page's stock holdings gave them each a personal wealth of about $4 billion. The IPO also turned approximately 1,000 of Google's 2,300 employees into millionaires.

Facing the Future

In the months following the IPO, some analysts worried that shareholders might pressure the company to earn greater profits, which could affect Google's corporate culture. Google's dominance of the search business also led to increased competition, as other powerful Internet companies entered the market. Microsoft founder Bill Gates vowed to develop new search products to cut into Google's lead, for instance, while Yahoo! ended its partnership with Google and launched its own new search engine. Google also faced increasing threats from "optimizers" — computer

*Employees at Google are encouraged to feel comfortable in the workplace,
as the contents of this office show.*

experts who used their understanding of the PageRank system to artificially raise the ranking of certain Web pages. Some users expressed concern that widespread optimization might reduce the quality of Google's search results.

Finally, Brin and Page had to make difficult decisions about what types of advertising to allow, what types of offensive material to censor, and what action to take against repressive governments that tried to block their citizens' access to Google. The founders tried to approach every decision with the best interests of Google users in mind. "We have a mantra: 'Don't be evil,' which is to do the best things we know how for our users, for our customers, for everyone," Page noted. "Obviously, everyone wants to be successful, but I want to be looked back on as being very innovative, very trusted and ethical, and ultimately making a big difference in the world," Brin added.

Over the years, Google Inc. has earned a reputation as a very innovative company in terms of the benefits it provides to employees. The company headquarters in Mountain View, California—called Googleplex—features a number of unusual workplace luxuries. The lobby holds a grand piano and a live projection of current search queries from around the world. Employees have unlimited access to workout facilities, yoga classes, a massage room, and pool and ping-pong tables. They can also eat three free meals per day in the company's cafeteria, which is headed by a gourmet chef. Finally, as a way to stimulate innovative thinking, Google encourages its employees to spend some of their time working on their own, original projects. "Engineers are supposed to spend 20 percent of their time doing whatever they want," Page explained. "That gets people working on things that they think are a good idea and that they're really excited about."

——— *"* ———

Partly due to the supportive atmosphere, Google has launched a series of innovative products over the years. Some of the notable innovations include the Google Toolbar, a downloadable browser plug-in that makes it possible to search with Google without visiting the home page; Google Zeitgeist, a periodic list of the top trending search terms; Local Search, a function that returns results within the user's community; and Gmail, a program that provides users with free email accounts and Web storage. "I think we've significantly raised the bar in Internet search, and I think we'll continue to do so," Page stated. "I don't see any limit to the significant innovations we can do to help people accomplish the tasks they're trying to do. We are quite optimistic that we can write interesting software that can make sense of information."

"We have a mantra: 'Don't be evil,' which is to do the best things we know how for our users, for our customers, for everyone," Page noted. "Obviously, everyone wants to be successful, but I want to be looked back on as being very innovative, very trusted and ethical, and ultimately making a big difference in the world," Brin added.

——— *"* ———

Technology reporter Steven Levy summed up the impact of Brin and Page's invention in *Newsweek:* "Because of its seemingly uncanny ability to provide curious minds with the exact information they seek, a dot-com survivor has supercharged the entire category of search, transforming the masses into data-miners and becoming a cultural phenomenon in the process," he wrote. "Google has become a high-tech version of the Oracle of Delphi, positioning everyone a mouseclick away from answers to the most arcane questions—and delivering answers so efficiently that the process becomes addictive."

THE BIN LADEN THREAT: WHAT CLINTON AND BUSH KNEW

Newsweek

March 29, 2004 $3.95

The Next Frontiers

The New Age of

Google

The Search Giant Has Changed Our Lives. Can Anybody Catch These Guys? By Steven Levy

PLUS: The Future of Digital Voting

Google Founders Larry Page and Sergey Brin

Advice to Young Inventors

Based on their own experiences as Internet entrepreneurs, Brin and Page offer the following advice to young inventors with a good idea: "You don't need to have a 100-person company to develop that idea," Page noted. "You can do it in your spare time, you can really work on ideas and see if they take off—rather than trying to raise tons of money, millions of dollars, for an idea that may or may not work. And once you have the product and people are using it, it's very easy to raise investment."

HOME AND FAMILY

Both Brin and Page are single. They both live in Palo Alto, California.

HOBBIES AND OTHER INTERESTS

In his spare time, Brin enjoys acrobatic sports. He has taken lessons in springboard diving and in flying trapeze. Page enjoys more earthbound pursuits like bicycling and in-line skating.

SELECTED HONORS AND AWARDS

Technical Excellence Award for Innovation in Web Application Development (*PC Magazine*): 1999
Top Ten Best in Cyberspace (*Time*): 1999
Best Search Engine (*Yahoo! Internet Life*): 2000
Best Search Engine (*The Net*): 2000
Webby Awards (International Academy of Digital Arts and Sciences): 2000, People's Voice Award and Best Technical Achievement; 2001, Best Practices; 2002, Best Practices, People's Voice Best Practices, and People's Voice Technical Achievement; 2003, People's Voice Technical Achievement and News; 2004, Best Practices, Services, People's Voice Best Practices, and People's Voice Services; 2005, Best Practices, People's Voice Best Practices, and Best Navigation/Structure

Best Internet Innovation (*PC Magazine*): 2000

Search Engine Watch Awards: 2001, for Outstanding Search Service and Most Webmaster Friendly Search Service; 2002, for Outstanding Search Service, Most Webmaster Friendly Search Service, Best Image Search Engine, Best Design, and Best Search Feature; 2003, for Outstanding Search Service; 2004, for Outstanding Search Service, Most Webmaster Friendly Search Service, Best News Search Engine, Best Image Search Engine, and Best Design

Pandia Award for Best All-Around Search Site: 2001, 2002

Net Awards: 2001, for Best Site and Best Search Engine

World Class Award (*PC World*): 2001, 2002, 2004

Global Leaders for Tomorrow (World Economic Forum): 2002

Innovator of the Year (*Research and Development*): 2002 (Page)

Marketer of the Year (*Adweek Magazine's Technology Marketing*): 2002 (Brin)

World's 100 Most Influential People (*Time*): 2004

National Academy of Engineering: 2004 (Page)

America's 25 Most Fascinating Entrepreneurs (*Inc.*): 2004

Greatest Innovators of the Past 75 Years (*Business Week*): 2004

World Technology Award for Best Marketing Communications: 2004

FURTHER READING

Books

Hillstrom, Kevin. *Defining Moments: The Internet Revolution*, 2005
Who's Who in America, 2005

Periodicals

Brandweek, Oct. 14, 2002
Current Biography Yearbook, 2001
Fortune, Nov. 8, 1999, p.298; Aug. 23, 2004, p.19; Dec. 13, 2004, p.98
Internet World, June 1, 2001, p.54
Lansing (MI) State Journal, Apr. 29, 2001, p.E1
Maclean's, May 8, 2000, p.46
New York Times, Feb. 1, 2004, p.C1; Aug. 20, 2004, p.C1
Newsweek, Dec. 16, 2002, p.46; Mar. 29, 2004, p.48; May 10, 2004, p.40
Online, May-June 2000, p.41
People, Aug. 23, 2004, p.77
Technology Review, Nov.-Dec. 2000, p.108
Time, Aug. 21, 2000, p.66
Washington Post, Feb. 22, 1999, p.F20; Oct. 28, 1999, p.E1

Online Articles

http://www.linuxgazette.com
  (*Linux Gazette,* "Interview with Google's Sergey Brin," Nov. 2000)
http://www.businessweek.com
  (*Business Week,* "Google's Larry Page: Good Ideas Still Get Funded,"
  Mar. 13, 2001; "Larry Page And Sergey Brin: Information At Warp
  Speed," Dec. 27. 2004)
http://www.wired.com
  (*Wired,* "Google vs. Evil," Jan. 2003)

Online Databases

Biography Resource Center Online, 2005, separate articles on Sergey Brin and
  Larry Page
WilsonWeb, 2005, article from *Current Biography,* 2001

ADDRESS

Sergey Brin and Larry Page
Google Inc.
1600 Amphitheatre Parkway
Mountain View, CA 94043

WORLD WIDE WEB SITES

http://www.google.com/corporate
http://www-db.stanford.edu/~sergey
http://www-db.stanford.edu/~page

Adam Brody 1980-

American Actor
Star of the Hit TV Series "The O.C."

BIRTH

Adam Jared Brody was born on April 8, 1980, in San Diego, California. His father, Mark Brody, is an attorney, and his mother, Valerie Brody, is a graphic designer. He has fraternal twin brothers, Matt and Sean, who are five years younger.

YOUTH

Brody had a fairly typical Southern California childhood. He enjoyed going to the beach and spent a great deal of his time surfing. "I lived 20 minutes inland, which was a travesty because I surfed every day," he stated. As a teenager, Brody pictured himself becoming a professional surfer someday, or at least owning a surf shop.

Brody always showed signs of being a natural performer. For example, he loved to tell jokes as a kid. Yet he never did any acting during his school years. In fact, his only early involvement in film came at the age of 18, when he made a surfing video featuring his friends. "It was sort of a painstaking process—this was before digital film, so everything had to be done through an editing machine," he recalled. He ended up screening the completed film at the local YMCA for an appreciative audience of about 200 people. "Everyone was cheering and yelling for everyone's waves," he remembered. "It was great. It was the most energy I've ever felt in a room. Surfer movies are great, because unlike regular movies you're supposed to scream and shout. It was like a concert with blasting music and everything. My parents were blown away."

EDUCATION

Brody attended Scripps Ranch High School in San Diego. "I did fine in high school," he related. "I was popular enough. I had friends, I dated. I don't have any high school horror stories." After graduating in 1998, he took classes at Mira Costa College in Oceanside, California. But Brody soon abandoned college in order to pursue a career as an actor.

CAREER HIGHLIGHTS

Becoming an Actor

After graduating from high school, Brody struggled to figure out what he wanted to do with his life. He ended up working as a clerk at a video store, which helped turn his attention toward acting as a potential career. "I got a job at Blockbuster in La Jolla, and it was incredibly boring," he recalled. "I was not into school, there wasn't anything I wanted to do. The only thing in my career counseling class that looked at all interesting was acting. I was kind of drifting."

As he catalogued movies and thought about the people who starred in them—many of whom were his own age—Brody decided to try his hand at acting. "On a whim, I told my best friend we should move to Los Angeles," he remembered. "[I told him,] 'We have no girlfriends, we have no internships, and we're not even at four-year schools. We can do anything right now. Let's take this opportunity while we have no strings. Let's go up and try it for a year.'" Brody convinced his parents to let him enroll in a college near Los Angeles. Then he used some of the money that was supposed to pay his college expenses to take acting classes and attend auditions.

Brody and his friend shared a tiny studio apartment in Santa Monica. "The room was L-shaped, and we had bunk beds in one end," he related. "It was so small, only one person could be vertical at a time. We had to take turns eating because one person would have to be lying down on the bed. It wasn't much bigger than a cell at juvenile hall." Brody took a series of odd jobs as a waiter, valet, and department store clerk to help pay the bills. Although it was difficult, he viewed this period as a necessary part of starting his new career. "I made a deal with myself," he explained. "I would come here and give myself one year, try acting my absolute hardest."

Brody's first acting job was a seven-line part on the daytime drama "The Young and the Restless" in 1999. A short time later, he received two lines of dialogue on the Saturday morning kids' show "City Guys." Although small, these parts helped make him more determined to be an actor. "[Acting] turned out to be something I love, and that I really feel is my calling," he stated. "I really feel like I lucked out and found something I love to do."

> "[Acting] turned out to be something I love, and that I really feel is my calling. I really feel like I lucked out and found something I love to do."

Shortly before his self-imposed one-year deadline, Brody received his first big break. He won the starring role in a made-for-TV movie called *Growing Up Brady,* which provided a behind-the-scenes look at the making of the hit 1970s series "The Brady Bunch." The movie was based on a tell-all memoir of the same name by Barry Williams, who played eldest son Greg Brady on the show. Brody played a dual role as the young actor Barry Williams and as Williams's TV character, Greg Brady. Although *Growing Up Brady* received generally poor reviews when it aired in 2000, it gave Brody some much-needed exposure. "Charmless acting, by-the-numbers directing, and a seemingly dashed-together script make for a thoroughly un-'Brady' experience," Phil Gallo wrote in *Variety.* The critic also acknowledged, however, that "Brody has some of the goofball charm of Greg's early years."

Growing Up Brady led to a series of acting jobs for Brody, which enabled him to quit his part-time jobs and focus all his attention on his new career. "I haven't had to have a job since then," he noted. In 2000 he appeared in the independent film *Never Land*. This modern retelling of the story of Peter Pan won several independent-film awards and was broadcast on PBS. Brody also had bit parts in *American Pie 2* (2001) and *The Ring* (2002). His biggest early film role came in *Grind* (2003), a comedy that follows four buddies from Chicago as they drive across the country to California in hopes of being discovered as professional skateboarders. Brody played Dustin, the uptight member of the group, who ends up financing the trip with his college fund. Unfortunately, *Grind* failed to connect with either audiences or critics.

Brody also earned several roles on television. He played Lucas on MTV's popular series "Undressed" and had a recurring role as Coop on the family drama "Once and Again." He attracted a following among teenaged girls in the recurring role of Dave Rygalski — boyfriend of Rory Gilmore's best friend, Lane — on the series "Gilmore Girls." Several critics claimed that Brody helped breathe new life and humor into the show.

"The O.C."

Brody received his ticket to stardom in 2003, when he was cast in a new TV series on the Fox network. The show was called "The O.C." in reference to Orange County, the area along the coast of California between Los Angeles and San Diego. The main story line concerns the Cohen family, led by idealistic attorney Sandy Cohen (played by Peter Gallagher). Working as a public defender, Sandy takes the case of Ryan Atwood (Benjamin McKenzie), a troubled teen from the rough neighborhood of Chino, California, who is accused of stealing a car. Sandy does not want to see Ryan put in prison or returned to his alcoholic mother, so he brings the boy home to his Newport Beach mansion. According to *Entertainment Weekly* writer Carina Chocano, however, Ryan "is just the kind of element the gates of the community were designed to keep out."

Sandy's desire to help Ryan creates a conflict with his heiress wife, Kirsten (Kelly Rowland), but she ultimately agrees to let the boy stay in their pool house. Their son Seth Cohen (played by Brody) immediately finds a kindred spirit in Ryan, and the teens become close friends. Despite his family's wealth, Seth too feels like an outsider among the shallow, image-conscious people who populate his high school and community — he is shy, naive, quirky, and somewhat nerdy, but also witty and endearing. Chocano described his character as "a nuanced portrait of a true-to-life dork, the odd product of the tension between his parents' ideology and their tax bracket." Writing in the *New Yorker*, Nancy Franklin added that "Brody is really too good-looking to be playing an unpopular kid, but he makes it

The cast of "The O.C.," from the first season.

work; he talks too much and too fast, he mumbles, and he projects zero physical confidence. In short, his character is adorable — except to people his own age."

Seth has a longstanding crush on Summer (Rachel Bilson), one of the most popular girls in his school. Unfortunately, Summer either treats Seth with contempt or pretends that he does not exist. Meanwhile, Ryan falls for the Cohens' troubled next-door neighbor, Marissa (Mischa Barton). The four teens' lives—as well as those of their parents—become intertwined in a web of dramatic story lines.

A Successful Series

"The O.C." made its debut during the summer of 2003—several weeks before the official start of the fall TV season. The pilot episode attracted an impressive 7.5 million viewers, and the series continued to gain viewers over the course of its first season to become one of the Fox network's biggest hits. It proved to be particularly popular among young people.

Critics also liked the show. While acknowledging that "The O.C." was basically a teen soap opera, many reviewers insisted that it had more to offer than typical shows in its genre. Chocano, for example, pointed out that "somewhere in all the high-stakes soapiness and often deft and subtle drama, there is a pretty wicked satire of baby-boomer values." Writing in *Time*, James Poniewozik admitted that he found the basic story line "predictable," but nevertheless noted that "'The O.C.' looks to have enough heart, talent, and wit to generate a few seasons' worth of luxurious suds." Reviewer Chuck Barney described it as "a crowd-pleasing show that not only contained all the requisite gloss and gorgeous faces, but offered fleshed-out characters—both teens and adults—along with touches of subversive wit and self-mockery."

> "When we first started, I had no inkling of how popular [Seth would] be. I was like, whatever, so I'm not the hot guy. Just don't dress me in anything too lame and I don't really care. I'm just gonna have my fun and do my job and screw around and whatever. And now it's weird. . . . I'm surprised at how many people feel like this character is speaking for them."

Brody attributed the show's success to the fact that it "blends different-aged characters, comedy, drama, reality, and heightened reality." He also claimed that viewers of all ages could identify with the characters and their dilemmas. "Everyone's felt uncool or like an outsider," he noted. "Everyone's been pushed to do something they didn't want to do. Maybe the exact details aren't the same, but the overall themes of the show are going to resonate." At the same time, Brody admitted that "The O.C." is enjoyable as

From the left: Marissa (Mischa Barton), Ryan (Benjamin McKenzie), Summer (Rachel Bilson), and Seth (Brody).

"classic TV escapism. . . . You watch the drama of these people living extravagant lives and then you see them go down."

Of all the characters on "The O.C.," Brody's Seth Cohen seemed to make the deepest connection with fans. Many teenagers identified with the sincere, socially awkward, geeky aspects of the character, while also wishing that they could fire off witty one-liners like Seth. "When we first started, I had no inkling of how popular he'd be," Brody admitted. "I was like, whatever, so I'm not the hot guy. Just don't dress me in anything too lame and I don't really care. I'm just gonna have my fun and do my job and screw around and whatever. And now it's weird. I've got people coming up to me saying, 'Seth Cohen is our hero.' I'm surprised at how many people feel like this character is speaking for them." Still, Brody insisted that Seth's awkwardness is a bit overstated. "We call him a geek because he's into comics and might wear a button-up," he noted. "But truthfully, is he that nerdy? Is he that socially inept? No, not really. He's just a little goofy and has a great sense of humor."

For Brody, the most realistic aspect of "The O.C." is Seth's relationship with his father, Sandy. "The big similarity between my life and the show is

The cast of "The O.C.," from the second season.

Seth's relationship with his dad. In high school, my dad had this ungodly standard for me getting all A's and B's. I would be like, I'm going to the party because the girl I like is there, and then he and I would fight," he recalled. "Now I look back and I don't know why I was so mean. He was right every time. It's hard because I think, Why is Seth turning his back on his dad?"

By all accounts, Brody also resembles his character in another way: his tendency to toss off quips and one-liners. In fact, the creator of "The O.C.,"

Josh Schwartz, has adjusted Seth's personality in order to take advantage of Brody's natural wit. "[I've] started to write this character in ways that allow Adam to put some of what we call his 'sauce' into the dialogue," Schwartz stated.

By the time the first season of "The O.C." concluded, several critics noted that Brody had emerged as the breakout star of the show. "Thanks to Mr. Brody's appealing acting . . . Seth all but hijacked the series last year," Ari Posner wrote in the *New York Times*. "His blend of smarts, unapologetic weirdness, and self-consciously romantic yearning transformed a potentially secondary character into such an attractive figure that he all but eclipsed the show's more obvious, more glamorous stars."

Enjoying Stardom

Brody is under contract to appear on "The O.C." for six seasons. The 25-year-old actor looks forward to the time when Seth and his friends will graduate from high school and move on with their lives. In the meantime, the popularity of the show has created a number of new acting opportunities for Brody. In 2003, for example, he co-starred with Ed Asner in the straight-to-video movie *Missing Brendan*. He played Patrick, a young man who travels to Vietnam with his grandfather in hopes of finding the remains of an uncle who died in the Vietnam War. In 2005 Brody earned a small but important role as Hector in *Mr. and Mrs. Smith,* a big-budget action-thriller starring Brad Pitt and Angelina Jolie. He is also scheduled to star opposite Meg Ryan in his first romantic comedy, *In the Land of Women.* His character is a screenwriter who travels from Los Angeles to suburban Michigan to care for his ailing grandmother, then becomes involved with the women who live across the street.

"I kind of missed out on a lot of what could've been an education. So now I'm always trying to educate myself. I won't put a TV in my trailer; I'm always reading books to fill in my gaps. I feel like I'm taking baby steps in this whole world of greater literacy, and I gotta say, I'm kind of proud of myself."

While Brody has enjoyed his rise to stardom, he claims that success has not spoiled him. "It's not so much that I can go buy that Ferrari I've always wanted or that white tiger," he explained. "It's more that I don't have to worry day to day. Now I'll get an appetizer or a glass of wine [at dinner]. I

Brad Pitt, Angelina Jolie, and Brody in a scene from Mr. and Mrs. Smith.

don't have to number crunch anymore." Brody hopes that he serves as inspiration to aspiring actors, helping them to believe that they can become successful through hard work. "If you really immerse yourself in Los Angeles and acting, if you go to acting class and start doing a good job, you're going to meet people who are agents, or who have agents," he noted. "It's almost unavoidable for anybody who wants to do it. Come up here, get in acting class, and get yourself out there. You make yourself known, and it will come to you, I think."

HOME AND FAMILY

Brody lives in an industrial-style loft apartment in West Hollywood with his dog, Penny, a pit-bull mix that he rescued from an animal shelter. He is single, although he has been linked romantically to his "O.C." co-star Rachel Bilson.

Brody remains close to his family, who have helped him remain grounded through his quick rise to stardom. "I will admit that I've caught myself about to act like a diva, totally," he noted. "But I try to check myself. When in doubt I look to my friends and family. They're so levelheaded, I figure if they're still hanging out with me I must be OK."

HOBBIES AND OTHER INTERESTS

In his spare time, Brody enjoys listening to music by indie bands like Interpol, Bright Eyes, and Death Cab for Cutie. He also plays drums in an alternative rock band called Big Japan. "Me and my friends are in a band, and it's fun," he said. "It's a great way to get out some aggression and it's just something that's really good and fun to put your energy into."

Brody also spends a lot of time reading—everything from comic books to nonfiction books about politics. "I kind of missed out on a lot of what could've been an education," he explained. "So now I'm always trying to educate myself. I won't put a TV in my trailer; I'm always reading books to fill in my gaps. I feel like I'm taking baby steps in this whole world of greater literacy, and I gotta say, I'm kind of proud of myself."

In addition, Brody watches a wide variety of movies on video, which helps him hone his craft as an actor. "I love movies. That's a big hobby," he stated. "I even love bad movies. Growing up, when I wasn't acting, I didn't want to watch bad movies. But now if it's bad, I notice other things [and think], 'OK, why did they put the camera there?' or 'What a horrible piece of dialogue.' Now, there are so many more things to look at."

SELECTED CREDITS

Television

Growing Up Brady, 2000
"Undressed," 2000
"Once and Again," 2000-01
"Gilmore Girls," 2002-03
"The O.C.," 2003-

Films

Never Land, 2000
American Pie 2, 2001
The Ring, 2002
Grind, 2003
Missing Brendan, 2003
Mr. and Mrs. Smith, 2005

HONORS AND AWARDS

Teen Choice Award: 2004, Favorite TV Actor in a Drama/Adventure

FURTHER READING

Books

Contemporary Theater, Film, and Television, Vol. 60, 2005
Krulik, Nancy. *Adam Brody: So Adorkable!,* 2004
Rizzo, Monica. *Meet the O.C. Superstars: The Official Biography!,* 2004
Zack, Elizabeth. *The Boys of Summer: The Unauthorized Biographies of
  Benjamin McKenzie and Adam Brody,* 2004

Periodicals

Boston Globe, Aug. 5, 2003, p.E6
Entertainment Weekly, Aug. 15, 2003, p.61; Sep. 5, 2003, p.43; Dec. 12, 2003,
  p.24; Nov. 5, 2004, p.34
New York Times, Oct. 31, 2004, Arts and Leisure, p.24
New Yorker, Aug. 18, 2003, p.144
Newsweek, Sep. 22, 2003, p.11
San Diego Union-Tribune, Aug. 5, 2003, p.E1
Teen People, Dec. 1, 2004, p.104; May 2005, p.110
Teen Vogue, Sep. 2004, p.165
Time, Aug. 11, 2003, p.63
Variety, May 15, 2000, p.39; Aug. 18, 2003, p.21
YM, Dec. 2003, p.74

Online Databases

Biography Resource Center Online, 2005, article from *Contemporary Theater,
  Film, and Television,* 2005

ADDRESS

Adam Brody
Fox Broadcasting Co.
P.O. Box 900
Beverly Hills, CA 90213

WORLD WIDE WEB SITES

http://www.fox.com/oc
http://www.kidzworld.com

Cornelia Funke 1958-

German Writer of Books for Children and
Young Adults
Author of *The Thief Lord, Inkheart,* and *Dragon Rider*

BIRTH

Cornelia Caroline Funke (pronounced FOON-keh) was born
in 1958 in Dorsten, Westphalia—a small, industrial town in
central Germany that she has described as "not very pretty"
and "a place you're a little bit bored by all the time." Her father was a lawyer, and her mother was a homemaker. She was
the oldest child in her family, with younger brothers and a
younger sister.

YOUTH

Funke was an imaginative child who loved to draw and paint. She often made up stories for her younger siblings, and she also loved to read fantasy and adventure tales—especially *The Chronicles of Narnia* by C.S. Lewis. "Most authors I read were British or American," she noted. Her father was also a great reader, and he often took her to the library. Despite her love of books and stories, however, Funke never really considered becoming an author. Instead, her early career plans included becoming an astronaut or a pilot. "Then I thought I wanted to marry a chief of a large American Indian nation and live with him and his people in the wide prairies," she recalled.

EDUCATION

Funke attended schools in Dorsten where, like most German students, she studied English for nine years. She has described herself as a good student but "not ambitious (which means quite lazy)." English was one of her favorite subjects, and she also "loved to write essays, though always too long and not always strictly on the topic."

At the age of 18 Funke moved to Hamburg, Germany. She earned a degree in education theory at the University of Hamburg, then completed coursework in book illustration at the Hamburg State College of Design. "I studied education (the most stupid idea of my life) because I wanted to work in some way with children, not as a teacher, but as a social worker," she related. "I think I wanted to make the world a better place, but I found out that you can't live against your gifts. And my gifts are writing and drawing."

CAREER HIGHLIGHTS

After completing her education, Funke began working with troubled children as a social worker. "I did work with children on an activity playground for a while, building huts and generally teaching them not to hit others as soon as they didn't get what they want," she remembered. Although Funke soon realized that the job would never make her completely happy, she did learn a great deal about the spirit and determination of children. "I still have the greatest respect for the little ones I met in those years—they all had bad, bad things to deal with, and did it so bravely," she noted. "I have often been impressed by children who come from very different social backgrounds: how much they care for siblings or friends, help each other, try to be strong."

Funke soon left social work and began applying her artistic talents as a designer of board games and illustrator of children's books. Dissatisfied with the quality of the stories she was asked to illustrate, she decided to start writing her own books. "I found that I am better at writing than illustrating, and more passionate about it," she stated. She sent her first effort, *The Great Dragon Quest,* to a German publisher in the mid-1980s. It was accepted immediately, and Funke launched a new career as an author of children's books. Over the next 15 years, Funke became one of Germany's most popular writers. She published more than 40 works, including picture books, early readers, chapter books, and young adult novels.

Herr der Diebe (The Thief Lord)

Although Funke speaks fluent English, she has written all of her books in German, her native language. To date, only a few have been translated into English. The first was *Herr der Diebe,* which was later published in English as *The Thief Lord.*

Funke first got the idea for *Herr der Diebe* during a visit with her family to Venice, Italy. She had always loved Venice — with its historic buildings, romantic atmosphere, and endless system of canals — and longed to share it with readers. "Venice is an enchanted place, but it is also very real — you can touch it, smell it, and taste it," she explained. "I wanted to tell children that there is a place in this world that is real and full of history, but also contains magic and mystery — not an imagined world, but right here, in a place they can visit."

> *"Venice is an enchanted place, but it is also very real — you can touch it, smell it, and taste it. I wanted to tell children that there is a place in this world that is real and full of history, but also contains magic and mystery — not an imagined world, but right here, in a place they can visit."*

The trip to Venice also brought back feelings from Funke's childhood, when she often wished that she could magically become an adult. "As far as I know, there is not one story about all those children who want to be an adult, so they can buy a dog at once, get a horse, or something else, watch movies all night or whatever, just have this freedom," she related. "So one day I had the idea of writing a story about a boy who has the same dream and who even pretends to be an adult."

Herr der Diebe tells the story of 12-year-old Prosper and his five-year-old brother, Boniface ("Bo"). When their mother dies, the boys are sent to live with their wealthy, cold-hearted aunt and uncle in Hamburg, Germany.

While the aunt is interested in raising cuddly Bo, she wants no part of the intense Prosper and plans to send him away to boarding school. Faced with the prospect of being separated, the boys run away to Venice, which their mother had once described to them as a magical city of moonlit canals. The orphans end up taking refuge in an abandoned movie theater with other street children. The leader of the street children is 12-year-old Scipio, who calls himself the Thief Lord. Dressed in boots and a mask like Robin Hood, Scipio steals jewels from rich people to support his young friends.

Publication in English

At first, *Herr der Diebe* and Funke's other works were popular primarily in Germany. That changed in 2002, when the book was first published in English. The translation was inspired by a bilingual girl named Clara, who spoke both German and English and had recently moved from Germany to England. She wrote a letter to Barry Cunningham, an editor at the British publisher Chicken House. He had become famous several years earlier as the editor who discovered J.K. Rowling's talent and published her "Harry Potter" series in England. In the letter, Clara asked Cunningham why her favorite book, *Herr der Diebe*, was not available in English translation. Cunningham contacted Funke's German publisher, read a translation that had been prepared by Funke's cousin, and immediately arranged to publish the book in English as *The Thief Lord*.

> *"It thrills me that English and American children will come to love the story as much as German children do, which proves that we are not that different,"* Funke stated.

The Thief Lord became an instant success, selling out its first printing in ten days in England, and reaching the number two spot on the *New York Times* children's bestseller list in the United States. It also won several awards in Europe, as well as the American Library Association's Mildred L. Batchelder Award as the best foreign-language children's book published in the United States in 2002. "It thrills me that English and American children will come to love the story as much as German children do, which proves that we are not that different," Funke stated.

In a review for *School Library Journal*, John Peters called *The Thief Lord* "a compelling tale, rich in ingenious twists, with a setting and cast that will linger in readers' memories." Writing for the *New York Times*, Rebecca Pepper Sinkler added that "There is magic here, but what lifts this radiant novel beyond run-of-the-mill fantasy is its palpable respect for both the struggle to grow up and the mixed blessings of growing old."

Exploring the World of Books with *Inkheart*

Following the success of *The Thief Lord*, Funke's young adult novel *Inkheart* was published in English in 2003. She drew upon her lifelong love of books in writing this story. "I have dreamed for a long time of writing a story in which characters from a book come into our world," she explained on her Web site. "Which book addict doesn't know the feeling that the characters in a book can seem more real than the people around us?"

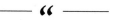

> "I have dreamed for a long time of writing a story in which characters from a book come into our world. Which book addict doesn't know the feeling that the characters in a book can seem more real than the people around us?"

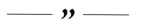

Inkheart tells the story of Meggie, a 12-year-old girl who lives with her father, Mo. Mo is a bookbinder who shares his love of books with his daughter. Unbeknownst to Meggie, however, Mo's connection with books goes much deeper than his job. He is a Silvertongue, meaning that he possesses an ancient gift that enables him to bring the characters of a book to life by reading their stories aloud. Unfortunately, when the book's characters come to populate the real world, real people also disappear into the pages of the book.

Nine years earlier, when Mo read the exciting novel *Inkheart* aloud to his wife, he had accidentally released the evil character Capricorn into the real world, while Meggie's mother had disappeared into the pages of the novel. Meggie learns about her father's secret when the mysterious Dustfinger, another character from *Inkheart*, shows up to ask Mo to read him back into the book. Her father is unable to reverse the process, however, and Meggie is soon drawn into an adventure rivaling any that she had read about.

Upon completing the novel, Funke sent a copy of the manuscript to Clara, the young fan whose letter had led to the English-language publication of *The Thief Lord*. Funke wanted Clara's input to make sure that her villains were not too frightening for young adults. "When I decided to do something with villains, I thought I'd like to do them really real and not fool children with evil, because they have to meet it at some time — it is not something abstract, like some stories depict," she explained. "I experience evil in the world as something very real and threatening." Clara responded that the villains were not too scary for her age group.

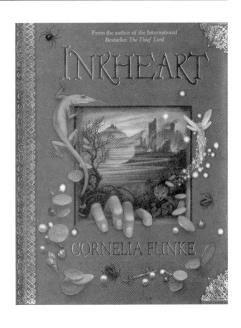

Inkheart quickly earned outstanding reviews. A writer for *Kirkus Reviews* called the novel "a true feast for anyone who has ever been lost in a book." A *Publishers Weekly* reviewer added that "Funke once again proves the power of her imagination; readers will be captivated by the chilling and thrilling world she has created here." Reviewer Jean Boreen noted in the *Journal of Adolescent and Adult Literacy* that "Funke does a wonderful job illuminating the difficulties faced by various characters as they choose between their own safety and that of a loved one, or debate the choices they might have to make to prove their loyalty to a friend. *Inkheart* will definitely catch the attention and admiration of most readers as it is, overall, a delightful read."

Funke has said that she found *Inkheart* the easiest to write among all of her books. In fact, once she had prepared an outline, the characters seemed to come to life and demand to tell their own stories. "I opened a door and all these characters ran out," she said. The vivid characters in her imagination eventually convinced Funke to expand *Inkheart* into a trilogy. "I love my characters to take me for a surprising ride," she explained. "You have to be confident enough to follow them. It is like walking to a cliff edge. . . . If you want to develop as a writer, you have to jump off — and fly." She planned to set the sequels mostly within the world that Dustfinger came from. "Dustfinger will go back home and some of the others will follow, either because they want to or because they are made to," Funke stated.

Writing Popular Children's Series

By the summer of 2004, Funke's books had sold five million copies in 28 countries around the world. Yet only a handful of her books had been translated into English by this time. In fact, one of her most popular series among German readers, *The Wild Chicks*, was not available in the United

States. This realistic fiction series features five books about a group of schoolgirls who call themselves "The Wild Chicks."

Another one of Funke's most popular books, *Dragon Rider*, made its American debut in 2004. This fantasy-adventure novel for young readers had helped establish Funke's reputation among German readers several years earlier. *Dragon Rider* tells the story of Firedrake, an unusual dragon who sets out to find the Rim of Heaven — the mythical home where dragons can live in peace forever. He is accompanied on his quest by a human boy named Ben, who turns out to be his dragon rider, and a feisty Scottish brownie girl named Sorrel. Along the way, they meet new friends but must also battle with the evil Nettlebrand, who is determined to exterminate all the world's dragons. "Exciting adventures abound, albeit counterbalanced with some implausible motivations, a few plot holes, and a dollup of syrupy sentiment," wrote Anita L. Burkam in *Horn Book.* "But for younger readers who want fantastical events straight up, . . . this book delivers." *Dragon Rider* reached the top position on the *New York Times* children's bestseller list shortly after its release.

Some of Funke's books for younger readers have recently been published in the United States. *The Princess Knight,* released in 2004, is a picture book about Violetta, a little princess whose father trains her to ride horses and engage in sword fights alongside her brothers. When she turns 16, however, the king insists that she behave like a traditional princess and marry the winner of a jousting contest. Determined to control her own destiny, Violet sneaks into the woods every night and trains herself to be the most clever, nimble knight in the kingdom. She competes in the jousting contest in disguise and wins her own independence. "Funke handles the picture book form just as deftly as her novels, with sure-footed pacing and a well-placed thrust through the cardboard princess stereotype," wrote a reviewer for *Publishers Weekly.* "Despite the fairy-tale surroundings, the heroine earns her triumph with believable determination, and readers young and old will root for her from start to finish."

> "There are people who know already at the age of six that they want to become a doctor or a teacher. Just don't worry if you're not one of these people. Take your time finding out what kind of work gives you so much joy that you could imagine doing it for the rest of your life. And then you can still change your mind completely halfway through your life and do something completely different. Why not?"

The popularity of Funke's books in English has led to several movie-production deals. *The Thief Lord, Inkheart,* and *The Wild Chicks* are all scheduled to be filmed in 2005. While Funke was thrilled at the prospect of see-

Funke and the actor Brendan Fraser surrounded by fifth-grade students at a book-signing for Inkheart.

ing her work on the big screen, she also expressed concern about the film-makers' ability to capture her artistic vision. "I get more and more the feeling that I should be very careful of the Hollywood influence," she stated. "Some people have given casting ideas that are just ridiculous. I don't want to make *Inkheart* with Jim Carrey or with Tom Hanks or with Brad Pitt [as Mo]. . . . If they do a movie that crushes the imagination, I'll never forgive myself. You write a book that you're passionate about and they spoil it!" Funke envisioned actor Brendan Fraser—star of *Gods and Monsters, The Mummy,* and *George of the Jungle*—in the role of Mo. In fact, she sent him a copy of *Inkheart,* and they ended up establishing a friendship. Fraser has since read some of Funke's books when they were recorded on audiotape.

Enjoying Her Work

Funke claims that she has more ideas for stories than she could ever write. "I have the feeling more and more that the story is just there and you have to find it," she stated. She spends about a year on a typical book, including six months of research and planning, followed by six months of writing and revising. Sometimes her books seem to write themselves. While she continues to illustrate some of her own books with line drawings, she no longer illustrates picture books by other authors.

Funke often reassures young people by telling them that it took her a while to discover her life's work. "I love my work. I love writing books and telling stories so much that I could not imagine doing anything else. But it took me a very long time to figure out that this was what I wanted to do, let alone that I could actually do it well enough to make a living from it," she explained. "Of course there are people who know already at the age of six that they want to become a doctor or a teacher. Just don't worry if you're not one of these people. Take your time finding out what kind of work gives you so much joy that you could imagine doing it for the rest of your life. And then you can still change your mind completely halfway through your life and do something completely different. Why not?"

Funke attributes her success as a writer partly to her ability to understand children and their interests. "I am an adult now, at least I look like one. But I still am amazed by the rituals and everything in the adult world and I still don't get it," she admitted. "Sometimes I feel like a spy for children, offering them a glimpse into the strange world of adults. The worst thing that can happen as an adult is to forget how the world felt when it was new."

Funke enjoys connecting with her young readers, especially those who share her deep love of books. "I like when a child comes to me at a reading and they have a book that looks like it's been read a dozen times," she stated. "A collector who brings me a book that is perfectly clean — that is kind of a creepy feeling. I feel like that book is dead. Nobody will ever touch it again. If I was a book, I would like to be a library book, so I would be taken home by all different sorts of kids. A library book, I imagine, is a happy book."

> *"I am an adult now, at least I look like one. But I still am amazed by the rituals and everything in the adult world and I still don't get it. Sometimes I feel like a spy for children, offering them a glimpse into the strange world of adults. The worst thing that can happen as an adult is to forget how the world felt when it was new."*

MARRIAGE AND FAMILY

Funke has been married to her husband, Rolf, for 25 years. Rolf worked as a book printer until his wife's writing career took off, then he quit his job to care for their children, Anna and Ben. Funke and her family live in the countryside north of Hamburg, Germany, in an older brick house "with a huge, wild garden, two horses, a guinea pig, and a hairy dog called Loony —because she is."

HOBBIES AND OTHER INTERESTS

One of Funke's hobbies is collecting dragons. "Ever since I wrote *Dragon Rider,* I have been a mad collector of dragons—stuffed dragons, paper dragons, china dragons, small ones, big ones, green ones, red ones—but there is still not a single one in my collection that can fly like Firedrake," she noted. In her spare time, she enjoys watching movies with her family and has an extensive collection of DVDs. Funke also lends her support to several German charities that serve underprivileged, ill, or refugee children.

SELECTED WRITINGS

The Thief Lord, 2002
Inkheart, 2003
The Princess Knight, 2004
Dragon Rider, 2004

HONORS AND AWARDS

Zurich Children's Book Award: 2000, for *The Thief Lord*
Venice House of Literature Award: 2001, for *The Thief Lord*
Notable Book Award (*New York Times*): 2002, for *The Thief Lord*
Mildred L. Batchelder Award (American Library Association): 2003, for *The Thief Lord*
Torchlight Prize (Askew Library Services): 2003, for *The Thief Lord*
Corinne 2003 International Book Award: 2003, for *The Thief Lord*
Children's BookSense Book of the Year: 2003, for *Inkheart*
Amelia Bloomer Project Award (American Library Association): 2005, for *The Princess Knight*

FURTHER READING

Periodicals

Bookseller, June 20, 2003, p.32
Buffalo (NY) News, Apr. 7, 2004, p.N6
Detroit Free Press, Dec. 5, 2002, Yak, p.2
Duluth (MN) News-Tribune, Jan. 7, 2004

Guardian (London), June 22, 2002, p.32; Oct. 29, 2003, p.17
Horn Book, Sep. 1, 2004, p.583
Journal of Adolescent and Adult Literacy, Sep. 2003, p.91; Feb. 2004, p.433
Kirkus Reviews, Sep. 15, 2003, p.1174
New York Post, Dec. 6, 2003, p.26
New York Times, Nov. 17, 2002, p.31
Observer (London), July 11, 2004, p.17
Publishers Weekly, July 21, 2003, p.196; Jan. 26, 2004, p.253
School Library Journal, Oct. 2002, p.163
Time, Apr. 18, 2005, p.120
USA Today, Sep. 5, 2002, p.D5
Variety, Oct. 20-26, 2003, p.12

Online Articles

http://www.bordersstores.com/features
 (Borders.com, "Hey American Kids, Meet Cornelia Funke," 2003)

Online Databases

Biography Resource Center Online, 2005, article from *Contemporary Authors Online,* 2005

Further information for this profile was taken from a National Public Radio interview with Funke, conducted Oct. 13, 2002.

ADDRESS

Cornelia Funke
Scholastic Inc.
557 Broadway
New York, NY 10012

WORLD WIDE WEB SITES

http://vbreitrein.layer2.de/projekt01 (click on the British flag for English translation)
http://www.doublecluck.com
http://www2.scholastic.com/teachers/authorsandbooks
http://www.bookbrowse.com

Pope John Paul II 1920-2005
Polish Religious Leader
Head of the Roman Catholic Church

[Editor's Note: John Paul II, the charismatic "people's pope" who helped topple Communism while championing Catholic values and the culture of peace, died on April 2, 2005. He died after a long struggle with illness that was characterized by his humble and graceful acceptance of suffering. His papacy was marked by his great personal popularity and the great esteem in which he was held by millions around the world. John Paul II was first profiled in Biography Today *in October 1992; this retrospective marks the occasion of his death.]*

BIRTH

Karol Jozef Wojtyla (pronounced voy-TIH-wuh), who adopted the name John Paul II when he became pope in 1978, was born May 18, 1920, in the market town of Wadowice in southern Poland. He was the second of two sons born to Karol Wojtyla, an administrative officer in the Polish Army, and Emilia (Kaczorowska) Wojtyla, a schoolteacher of Lithuanian descent. His brother, Edmund, was 15 years his senior.

YOUTH

Like most of the population of Poland, where people are known for their fierce devotion to the Catholic Church, the Wojtylas were a deeply religious family who prayed together and went to mass every day. In fact, the building that housed their modest apartment was located in the shadow of the 600-year-old Cathedral of St. Mary in Wadowice, where young Karol was baptized a month after his birth. Karol was not particularly pious as a boy, however, and his early years provided little indication that he would eventually enter the priesthood.

The Wojtylas lived a simple life, as did most of the people in their town, and Karol divided his time among school, church, and outdoor play. He was an athletic child who loved every imaginable sport, from the street game *palant* (played with two sticks), to soccer, to swimming and canoeing. His favorite sport, though, was skiing, and he practiced on the hills around his home until he was old enough to go to the steep slopes of the nearby Tatra mountains.

Karol's boyhood was marred by sadness. His beloved mother died when he was barely nine years old. Then tragedy struck again a few years later when his brother Edmund, by then a physician, died after contracting scarlet fever from a patient. From this time on, father and youngest son were left to fend for themselves. The senior Karol's military background made him a strict parent who expected obedience, but he was a warm father as well. Friends from those days remember the special bond forged between the elder Wojtyla and his son. The two attended mass every morning and often strolled the streets together after their evening meal. During these years, they lived frugally on a small army pension, with the retired father doing all of the washing, mending, and cooking. He also guided his son in his studies and checked the boy's schoolwork each day.

EDUCATION

Young Karol Wojtyla was a good student from the time he entered primary school at the age of seven, but it was in the upper grades that he excelled.

A young Karol Wojtyla, age two, with his father in a formal portrait taken in Krakow, Poland.

His father chose to send him to the state high school for boys rather than to either of the private schools in Wadowice. During high school, Karol's interests broadened to include literature and drama, Latin, poetry, and music. He loved acting, too, and his friends and teachers felt that he would one day choose the theater as his profession. The church remained a major part of his life, though, and he continued to serve as an altar boy, as he had done in his very young years, and also headed a student religious society. After high school, Karol enrolled at Krakow's ancient Jagiellonian University. His studies revolved around language and literature, but he also was a prominent member of a drama group.

World War II

Wojtyla's life as a student was interrupted a year later by the beginning of World War II. Germany invaded Poland on September 1, 1939, and soon closed all universities. In *The People's Pope*, James Oram discussed the goal of the Third Reich, as the Nazi government was known. "The Germans were determined," Oram explained, "to wipe out all Polish intellectual thought because they saw the Poles only as slaves and there was no room in the plans of the Reich for those who studied, debated, and questioned."

Young Karol was issued a work card by the Germans after their invasion of his country and forced to labor in a limestone quarry outside Krakow. He spent three years at the backbreaking job, and his meager pay was the only income to support him and his father, whose military pension had been cut off when war broke out. During this time, Karol attended informal classes at night wherever young students could hide from the Nazis, and he began to write memorable and touching poetry. He also helped an old friend form an underground drama group, the Rhapsodic Theater, which would play to small audiences in secret in an effort to keep Polish pride alive.

Studying for the Priesthood

Several biographers claim that Karol Wojtyla's calling to the priesthood began with the unexpected death of his cherished father in 1941. At that time, the horrors of war were everywhere: innocent people were snatched away in the night, never to be seen again, and rumors had begun to circulate about the Nazi gas chambers at Auschwitz, not far from Krakow, where millions of Jews were murdered. Although these tragedies undoubtedly influenced his decision, Wojtyla rarely spoke openly about this period of time, when "the most important questions of my life were born and crystallized," he revealed, "and the road of my calling was decided." Upon deciding to become a Roman Catholic priest, Wojtyla continued his studies at a secret and illegal "seminary" at Cardinal Adam Sapieha's palace in Krakow.

After the war ended, Wojtyla finally was able to return to his studies. He was ordained as a priest on November 1, 1946, and sent to study at the Angelicum, or Papal University, in Rome. He received a doctorate of divinity from this institution in 1948. After returning from Rome, he was assigned to a small village church. But within a year he was back in Krakow at the Jagiellonian University, which had reopened after the war. He eventually earned two PhD degrees from the Jagiellonian, in ethics and phenomenology—the study of human consciousness and self-awareness. When he received his second doctorate, he was appointed to the faculty at the university.

CAREER HIGHLIGHTS

Serving the Catholic Church

Wojtyla began his priestly duties around the time that the Soviet Union evicted the Nazis from Poland and installed a Communist government there. The ruling Communists took a hostile view toward religion and shut down many Catholic institutions in Poland. In 1954, Wojtyla began to teach at the Catholic University of Lublin, the only Catholic institution of higher learning in Poland that had not been shut down by the Communists. He soon became head of its ethics department. Around this time, several religious leaders were arrested under trumped-up charges of "disloyalty" to the Polish nation. The popular Cardinal Stefan Wyszynski was among them. After his release in 1956, however, Wyszynski was able to effect a degree of church autonomy unrivaled in any other Communist country by agreeing that the church would not become involved in politics.

Religion in Poland thrived afterward, and it was during these years that Wojtyla began his rise through the ranks of Polish church leaders. He be-

Pope John Paul II making his first official appearance as pope, October 1978.

came auxiliary bishop of Krakow in 1958. Two years later he went to Rome for the Second Vatican Council, the first general assembly of Catholic Church leaders in nearly a century. Under the guidance of the beloved Pope John XXIII, Vatican II announced a modernization and liberalization of church practices. It was here that Bishop Wojtyla "first established the international regard and contacts that were to make him pope," according to *Time* magazine.

More church honors followed. In 1964 Wojtyla was named archbishop of Krakow, and in May 1967, at the age of 47, he became the second-youngest cardinal in Vatican history. As cardinal, he moved easily in the elite circles of the Vatican, the independent state within the borders of Rome that houses the headquarters of the Catholic Church. When Pope Paul VI, successor to John XXIII, died in August 1978, Cardinal Wojtyla was among those who voted for a new pontiff. The cardinals chose from among themselves the gentle and fragile Albino Luciani of Italy, who became Pope John Paul I.

Only one month into his papacy, however, Pope John Paul I died. The College of Cardinals convened again and, this time, did the unexpected. After several attempts to decide between the two leading Italian candidates resulted in a deadlock, they elected the first non-Italian pope since 1522, Karol Wojtyla of Poland. *Time* called him "the first international pope to lead the global church" and "a man of extraordinary qualities and experience." Out of respect for the recently deceased pope—and also because of his reverence for Paul VI, whom he called "my inspiration and strength"—Wojtyla chose the name John Paul II.

Spreading His Message around the World

Almost immediately upon being elected pope, John Paul demonstrated his determination to spread the message of Catholicism around the world. As Robert D. McFadden wrote in the *New York Times*, "Almost from the start, it was evident to many of the world's Roman Catholics, and to multitudes of non-Catholics, that this was to be an extraordinary papacy, one that would captivate much of humanity by sheer force of personality and reshape the church with a heroic vision of a combative, disciplined Catholicism." He launched an ambitious series of overseas trips that, over the course of his 26-year papacy, made him the most-traveled pope in history. He eventually made more than 100 trips abroad and visited 129 different countries. His journeys, which covered nearly 690,000 miles, ensured that he was seen and heard in person by more people than any other public figure in history. "He was determined from the start to make the world his parish and go out and minister to its troubles and see to its spiritual needs," McFadden explained. "He saw himself primarily as a spiritual figure who transcended geographical and ideological boundaries, and he saw it as his mission to deliver a clear set of Catholic ideas and to foster peace and human dignity through the power of faith."

> *As Robert D. McFadden wrote in the* New York Times, *"Almost from the start, it was evident to many of the world's Roman Catholics, and to multitudes of non-Catholics, that this was to be an extraordinary papacy, one that would captivate much of humanity by sheer force of personality and reshape the church with a heroic vision of a combative, disciplined Catholicism."*

Some of John Paul's travels had far-reaching political effects. His first official visit to his homeland in 1979, for example, is widely credited with helping to topple Communism in Eastern Europe. Although the Communist government that ruled Poland tried to mute the impact of the pope's visit — by refusing to allow him to speak in large cities or to give workers time off to hear him — he was nonetheless met by huge, enthusiastic crowds. The large turnout — estimated at 13 million people during his 10-day visit — demonstrated that Poles were largely united in their discontent with the Communist government. This revelation gave some Polish leaders the courage to launch a democratic revolution.

One year after John Paul's visit, Polish dockworkers ignored Communist rules and started a trade union movement called Solidarity. The pope repeatedly expressed his support for Solidarity over the next few years, and the popular movement grew steadily in strength and influence. In 1989 Poland held free elections and the Solidarity party won an overwhelming victory, ending 40 years of Communist rule. The fall of Communism in Poland soon encouraged similarly successful movements in Germany and the Soviet Union. Although many historians credit the pope with aiding the fall of Communism, John Paul was reluctant to accept responsibility for the wave of democracy that swept across Eastern Europe. "The tree was already rotten," he once said. "I just gave it a good shake and the rotten apples fell."

> **Although many historians credit the pope with aiding the fall of Communism, John Paul was reluctant to accept responsibility for the wave of democracy that swept across Eastern Europe. "The tree was already rotten," he once said. "I just gave it a good shake and the rotten apples fell."**

In all of his public appearances, the pope charmed crowds with his personal warmth and enthusiasm. He would charge into the crowds to talk to people, reaching out to touch them. In return, they offered their affection and trust. John Paul was fluent in seven languages (Polish, Latin, Italian, French, German, Spanish, and English) and conversant in several others, which allowed him to connect with people around the world in their native tongues. His charismatic presence on the world stage helped broaden the geographic and ethnic diversity of the Catholic Church and increase membership from 750 million to more than 1 billion. His travels also focused world attention on the problems of poverty and repression affecting the people of many countries. He gained a worldwide reputation as a champion of human rights and human dignity, providing a voice for people throughout the world who are poor, oppressed, victimized, and powerless.

The pope was greeted warmly wherever he went, especially among children.

John Paul's penchant for traveling and meeting with followers once nearly cost him his life. On May 13, 1981, the pope became the target of an assassination attempt. As he circled St. Peter's Square in the white vehicle that the press had dubbed "the popemobile," a man fired several shots at him. The bullets hit John Paul in the abdomen, right arm, and left hand. He underwent five hours of surgery to repair the damage. His assailant was Mehmet Ali Acga, a Turk already wanted for murder in his own country. Agca was believed to have been an agent of the Bulgarian government, a Communist regime that resented the pope's unbending stance against repression. The pope eventually forgave Acga and visited him in prison. Security around the pope was tightened in the ensuing years, but John Paul often defied attempts to keep him from potentially dangerous situations.

Just as he had reached out to Catholics around the world, the pope used his position to improve relations between the Church and other major religions. As a witness to the horrors of the Holocaust, John Paul made it a priority of his papacy to forge stronger ties with the Jewish people. He emphasized the ancient connections between Christianity and Judaism, for example, and he issued an apology for the failure of some Catholics to aid Jews during the Holocaust. In 1986 John Paul II made a historic visit to

65

The pope prays at the Western Wall, Judaism's holiest site, during his historic visit to Jerusalem.

Israel, where he became the first pope to pray in a synagogue and placed a note in Jerusalem's Western Wall. In 1993, the Vatican formally recognized the state of Israel, which was formed after World War II and the Holocaust to serve as a homeland for the world's Jews. John Paul made similar efforts to improve relations with Muslims. In a historic visit to the Middle East in 2001, for instance, he became the first pope ever to set foot inside a mosque.

Defending Conservative Traditions

Traveling and spreading his message of peace and hope around the world was just one part of John Paul's legacy. From the beginning of his tenure, the pope also embarked on a mission to "solidify the foundations of Catholicism, which he believed were beginning to crumble under the weight of the modern age," according to biographer Timothy Walch. Schooled in the staunchly conservative Catholic Church of Poland, John Paul steadfastly defended the traditional moral authority of Church doctrine throughout his papacy. He repeatedly called "for a return to traditional Catholic ethical values: he condemned homosexuality as morally wrong; he called on priests to honor their vows of obedience and celibacy; he told the laity that premarital sex, contraception, and abortion were repugnant, . . . and he put severe limits on Catholic academic freedom and theological inquiry," Walch noted. "Pope John Paul II was a man who used the tools of modernity to struggle against the modern world," an editorial stated in the *New York Times*. "He traveled more than a half-million miles through 129 countries, waving to crowds from his popemobile. He wrote best sellers and took advantage of every means of communication to spread his message: a cry against what he saw as the contemporary world's moral decadence, moral degradation, and abandonment of values."

"Pope John Paul II was a man who used the tools of modernity to struggle against the modern world," an editorial stated in the **New York Times.** *"He traveled more than a half-million miles through 129 countries, waving to crowds from his popemobile. He wrote best sellers and took advantage of every means of communication to spread his message: a cry against what he saw as the contemporary world's moral decadence, moral degradation, and abandonment of values."*

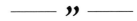

Some supporters appreciated the pope's conservative stance on social issues, viewing him as a rock of moral values in a confused world. But more liberal Catholics, especially in the United States, questioned some of John Paul's teachings — especially his rejection of birth control, his refusal to address a chronic shortage of priests by allowing priests to marry, and his refusal to allow the ordination of female priests to give women an equal voice in the church. These dissenters felt that the pope was out of touch with the modern world and argued that his conservative stances held back social progress. In fact, some American Catholics adopted a "cafeteria" approach to religion, observing the parts that suited their lifestyles and ignoring others.

Over the years, many observers commented on John Paul's demand for loyalty and intolerance for dissent within the Church. He took a number of steps to centralize authority in the Vatican, rather than allowing individual parishes to choose their own approaches. In fact, he drew criticism by dismissing a number of bishops and cardinals who did not agree with his conservative philosophy. "He was a pope who thought you could deal with the confusion after the Second Vatican Council — the inevitable, necessary confusion of growth and change — by putting a lid on it, by clamping down, by tightening things up," Father Andrew Greeley asserted. "This didn't work. It was the wrong strategy applied by a great man."

Criticism of John Paul's handling of internal affairs peaked in 2002, when he finally took steps to address a sex abuse scandal that had been brewing for many years. Since the 1950s, there had been thousands of allegations in the United States of young children being sexually abused by Catholic priests. In Boston alone, for example, approximately 1,000 children were sexually abused by pedophile priests. In some cases, bishops had tried to cover up suspected incidents of abuse by transferring the accused priests to other parishes — where they would be free to continue the pattern of abuse on a new group of unsuspecting children. In 2002 the pope ordered the release of Church documents detailing abuse allegations and adopted a zero-tolerance policy toward sexual abuse. He authorized the payment of reparations to confirmed victims, and he also condemned offenders, calling sexual abuse an "appalling sin" and saying that there was "no place in the priesthood or religious life for those who would harm the young." Still, some critics claimed that John Paul had not acted swiftly enough to protect young Catholics from abuse, while others claimed that his focus on the global stage had caused him to neglect internal problems. Overall, the crisis challenged the moral authority of the church in the eyes of many Americans.

Declining Health and Death

Over the course of John Paul's 26-year pontificate, the world watched as the pope's health underwent a gradual decline. He started his tenure as a robust 58-year-old skier and mountain-climber who insisted on building a lap pool inside the Vatican for his daily exercise. In his later years, however,

Millions of mourners poured into Rome and Vatican City to mark the passing of the pope.

he became increasingly frail until he was barely able to carry out his duties. "His physical decay unfolded before the eyes of a world both dazzled by his will and sometimes aghast at the cruelty of a vocation that would impose such burdens," John L. Allen, Jr., wrote in the *National Catholic Reporter.* "The pope struggled to walk, he slurred his speech and drooled badly, his hearing failed, and his facial expression became increasingly frozen. Yet he soldiered on, bearing his thorns in the flesh with grit and good humor."

The pope's decline began in 1992, when doctors removed a cancerous tumor from his abdomen. Over the next few years, he suffered a series of falls that resulted in broken bones. By 1999 he had grown so frail that he needed a cane, and the Vatican acknowledged that he was suffering from both arthritis and Parkinson's disease, a progressive neurological disorder that causes tremors and paralysis. By 2002 his symptoms were so severe that he could no longer walk, and aides either carried him or pushed him in a wheelchair. Still, the pope continued writing, traveling, and making public appearances almost until the end of his life. Throughout his courageous struggle with failing health, John Paul became an international symbol of aging with dignity.

In early 2005 the pope began to experience problems with his kidneys and lungs, and he was hospitalized several times with fevers and infections. He spent his final days in his papal apartment in the Vatican, attended by friends and colleagues. Thousands of followers maintained a prayerful vigil in the courtyard outside. Pope John Paul II died on April 2, 2005, at the age of 84. An estimated 4 million pilgrims came to Rome to mourn his death, some of whom stood in line for up to 24 hours just to get a glimpse of the pope's body. In addition, mourners filled churches around the world, testifying to the pope's deep personal popularity on the international stage. At his funeral, an impressive array of current and former world leaders gathered to pay their respects, as millions more thronged the streets of Rome.

> **"He was a magnificent pope who presided over a controversial pontificate, at turns daring and defensive, inspiring and insular," wrote John L. Allen, Jr. "[John Paul II] leaves behind the irony of a world more united because of his life and legacy, and a church more divided."**

The passing of a pope sets in motion a series of events that are dictated by centuries of tradition. For instance, within a short time the 117 members of the College of Cardinals travel to the Vatican and lock themselves in the Sistine Chapel to elect a new pope. They chose Cardinal Joseph Ratzinger of Germany, who had served as one of John Paul II's closest aides. Cardinal Ratzinger chose to be known as Pope Benedict XVI. One of his first acts was to set aside the usual five-year waiting period in order to put his predecessor on a "fast track" to sainthood.

The obituaries that appeared following the death of the pope provided a mixed assessment of John Paul's legacy. Many observers noted the charismatic appeal that made him popular among people of faith around the world. "Bells tolled solemnly across the continents, prayers and hymns filled great cathedrals and modest churches, and around the world mourning multitudes remembered Pope John Paul II . . . as the torchbearer of peace and human dignity, a tireless traveler whose journey finally ended," wrote Robert T. McFadden. But other observers were more critical of his resistance to change and modernization within the Church. "He was a magnificent pope who presided over a controversial pontificate, at turns daring and defensive, inspiring and insular," John L. Allen, Jr. wrote. "[John Paul II] leaves behind the irony of a world more united because of his life and legacy, and a church more divided."

One expert on the Vatican, Giancarlo Zizola, summarized his legacy like this: "This pope will have a place in history. Not just for what he is glorified for now, for attracting the great masses, as a sporty pope — this won't last. Not even the fall of the Berlin Wall, the defeat of Communism, because he himself said it would destroy itself. But he will be remembered for the seeds he laid. He will be remembered for his great favoring of dialogue between different religions, for the culture of peace, and the courage to speak against wars. For having saved the values of the West from the West itself. And the human form he gave to the papacy. It is not negative or positive: it is a complete pontificate."

SELECTED WRITINGS

Pope John Paul II published more than one million words in his lifetime. He authored hundreds of books, essays, articles, and poems, as well as encyclicals (papal documents) defining the religious, moral, and political policy of the Catholic Church. The following selections are among his best-known works or those intended for a juvenile audience.

Crossing the Threshold of Hope, 1994
Pope John Paul II: In My Own Words, 1998
My Dear Young Friends: Pope John Paul II Speaks to Teens on Life, Love and Courage, 2000
For the Children: Words of Love and Inspiration from His Holiness John Paul II, 2000
Every Child a Light: The Pope's Message to Young People, 2002
The Poetry of Pope John Paul II, 2003
Lessons for Living, 2004

HONORS AND AWARDS

Smithson Medal (Smithsonian Institution): 1979
Olympic Order (International Olympic Committee): 1981
Man of the Year (*Time*): 1994

FURTHER READING

Books

Bernstein, Carl, and Marco Politi. *His Holiness: John Paul II and the Hidden History of Our Time,* 1996
Fischer, Heinz-Joachim, and others. *Pope John Paul II: A Pope for the People,* 2004

Kwitny, Jonathan. *Man of the Century: The Life and Times of Pope John Paul II,* 1997

Oram, James. *The People's Pope: The Story of Karol Wojtyla of Poland,* 1979

Sullivan, George. *Pope John Paul II: The People's Pope,* 1984

Walch, Timothy. *Pope John Paul II,* 1989

Weigel, George. *Witness to Hope: The Biography of Pope John Paul II,* 1999

Who's Who in America, 2005

Wilson, Jay. *Pope John Paul II,* 1992 (juvenile)

Wilson, M. Leonora. *Karol from Poland: The Life of Pope John Paul II for Children,* 1999 (juvenile)

Wolfe, Rinna. *The Singing Pope: The Story of John Paul II,* 1980 (juvenile)

Periodicals

Catholic New Times, Apr. 24, 2005, p.4

Christian Century, Oct. 14, 1987, p.876; Oct. 12, 1988, p.887; Apr. 19, 2005, pp.8, 12

Christian Science Monitor, Apr. 4, 2005, p.1

Commonweal, Oct. 7, 1988, p.516

Los Angeles Times, Apr. 3, 2005, p.A1

National Catholic Reporter, Apr. 15, 2005, p.3

New York, Oct. 30. 1978, p.93

New York Times, Apr. 3, 2005, pp.A1, A39, A46 (multiple articles); Apr. 9, 2005, p.A1

New York Times Biographical Service, May 1979, p. 614; Oct. 1982, p.1331; May 1985, p.549

New Yorker, Oct. 17, 1994, p.50

Newsweek, Oct. 30, 1978, p.78; May 25, 1981, p.24; Apr. 11, 2005 (multiple articles); Apr. 18, 2005 (multiple articles)

Time, Oct. 30, 1978, p.84; May 25, 1981, p.10; Jan. 9, 1984, p.27; Apr. 11, 2005 (multiple articles); Apr. 18, 2005 (multiple articles)

Times (London), Apr. 4, 2005, Features, p.50

USA Today, Apr. 8, 2005, p.A14

Washington Post, Apr. 3, 2005, pp.A1, A31, B6 (multiple articles)

WORLD WIDE WEB SITE

http://www.vatican.va

Wangari Maathai 1940-
Kenyan Environmentalist, Feminist, Human Rights
Activist, and Educator
Winner of the 2004 Nobel Peace Prize

[Editor's Note: Wangari Maathai first appeared in Biography
Today *in 1997. Since then, she has continued to distinguish herself
as an internationally known environmental and political activist
and was named the winner of the 2004 Nobel Peace Prize. This
entry covers her life to date, with a special focus on her accomplish-
ments since the late 1990s.]*

BIRTH

Wangari Muta Maathai (pronounced wan-GAH-ree mah-DHEYE) was born Wangari Muta on April 1, 1940, in Nyeri, a town in south-central Kenya, about 60 miles north of Nairobi, the country's capital. She later lived near the towns of Solai and Kanungu. Her family was part of the Kikuyu people, one of the many cultural groups that live in east-central Africa. She has described her parents as "very simple farmers" and said that her father was "a squatter on a white settler's farm." This means that her family worked and lived on land that they did not own, though she also said her father was on good terms with the landowner. Her family practiced subsistence farming. In other words, the food they raised was primarily used to feed their family, rather than being sold as a cash crop. Her father also served as farm mechanic. Of the family's six children, Maathai was the oldest daughter.

BACKGROUND ON KENYA

At the time Maathai was born, Kenya did not exist as an independent country. Instead, the area, known as British East Africa, was a colony ruled by the United Kingdom. The British had entered the region in the mid-1800s and established large agricultural plantations and other businesses. This region, and indeed all of Africa, was fundamentally transformed by colonialism. The colonial rulers regarded most aspects of African life as inferior to those of Europe. They tried to change the Africans' way of life, imposing their own social customs, languages, and religious beliefs. The Europeans also erected governments and legal systems that ensured that they would maintain political and economic power over the Africans. They took Africa's land and natural resources for themselves, accumulating great wealth in the process, but they shared little of this wealth with Africans. Instead, Africans were herded into the colonies' most difficult and lowest-paying jobs.

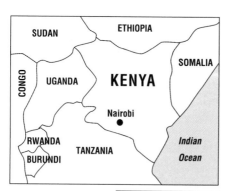

ABOVE: Closeup of Kenya and surrounding countries.

RIGHT: Kenya in relationship to the continent of Africa.

Under British rule, the African residents of British East Africa were forced into a social and economic position below that of the colonists. Some worked as laborers on the plantations, while others maintained their own small farms. Beginning in the late 1940s, colonized people all around the world began to demand their independence in the aftermath of World War II. In British East Africa, Jomo Kenyatta (1891?-1978) led the battle to end British rule. After several years of fighting, the independence forces triumphed, and in 1963, the country of Kenya was created. Kenyatta became the country's first prime minister and later its president. His political party, the Kenya African National Union (KANU), dominated the country's government for the next 40 years. (For more information on Kenyatta, see *Biography Today World Leaders Series,* Vol. 2: *Modern African Leaders.*)

At the time Maathai grew up, it wasn't common for a Kenyan girl to receive an education. But her family had an eye toward the future. "My parents were progressive people," she said, "and they decided that I should have a chance to go to school."

MAATHAI'S EDUCATION

At the time Maathai grew up, it wasn't common for a Kenyan girl to receive an education. But her family was looking toward the future. "My parents were progressive people," she said, "and they decided that I should have a chance to go to school." Maathai began attending classes when she was eight years old, enrolling at Ihithe Primary School near her home in Kanungu. She later studied at Mathari Girls Intermediate School, and in 1955 she entered Loreto Convent Limuru Girls High School. She did very well in her studies, and her teachers singled her out as a promising student.

As Maathai was finishing her high school studies in the late 1950s, her homeland was moving toward independence. Maathai's education suddenly became joined with her country's political future. Surprisingly, it all began in another part of the world. A group of United States politicians, which included John F. Kennedy, started a program to bring gifted Africans to America to receive a college education. They hoped this program would develop future leaders who would help guide the newly independent African countries. Maathai was chosen to be part of the program, and in 1960, she moved to the United States. The trip to the U.S. included her first airplane trip and her first ride on an escalator, where she lost her shoe.

Then she took a Greyhound bus from New York City to Atchison, Kansas, and enrolled at Mount St. Scholastica College.

"I'd never seen so much flat land or so much corn," Maathai said of her new home on the plains. The school was operated by members of the Benedictine religious order, and she was inspired by the nuns that taught her. "On a daily basis, I saw women working hard for higher goals and inner peace," she later recalled. "This must have impacted my own conscience and values as I matured." She graduated with a Bachelor of Science (BS) degree in biology in 1964. She then entered a post-graduate program at the University of Pittsburgh, where she earned a Master of Science (MS) degree in biological science in 1966. Next, she attended the University of Munich in Germany for a short time, but she began to feel the pull of her homeland once again. Believing that she "had to go back home . . . and make a contribution," she returned to Kenya in 1966. She took a job shortly after she arrived, but she wasn't finished with college. She enrolled in a doctoral program at the University of Nairobi, and in 1971 she received a doctoral degree (PhD) in anatomy. She was the first woman in all of eastern and central Africa to earn a doctorate.

> *At the University of Nairobi, many of her colleagues weren't happy to have a female in their ranks. "The typical African woman is supposed to be dependent, submissive," Maathai explained. Some men questioned the education she had received in the United States. "They wondered if it was really a master's degree or if it was just a joke," she said.*

CAREER HIGHLIGHTS

Maathai chose to work in the field of veterinary medicine, which allowed her to assist the many people in Kenya who raise livestock. When she first returned to Kenya, she took a position as a research assistant in the department of veterinary medicine at the University of Nairobi in 1966; she remained with the school for the next 16 years. Many of her colleagues weren't happy to have a female in their ranks. "The typical African woman is supposed to be dependent, submissive," Maathai explained. Some men questioned the education she had received in the United States. "They wondered if it was really a master's degree or if it was just a joke," she said.

Maathai didn't let sexism stand in her way. After earning her PhD, she became chair of the university's Department of Veterinary Anatomy in 1976 and was appointed associate professor in 1977. She was the first woman to hold these positions at the university. "Others told me that I shouldn't have a career, that I shouldn't raise my voice, that women are supposed to have a master," she explained. "Finally I was able to see that if I had a contribution I wanted to make, I must do it, despite what others said."

A Changing Environment

One of Maathai's projects at the university was to conduct research about ticks that infested livestock. In the process, she found a more basic issue. "When I spoke to farmers, their real problems were not the tick but

Maathai's book tells the story of the Green Belt Movement: its history, organization, objectives, and philosophy. The book also explains how to start a similar organization devoted to environmental and social justice issues.

the availability of water, the productivity of the soils, and the shortage of fuelwood," she said. These conversations made her reflect on a change she had noticed in Kenya. Upon her return to the country after six years studying abroad, she found that there were far fewer trees. This condition is known as deforestation—the removal of forests. Also, there was less ground water than in previous decades. "I noticed springs that I knew as a child drying up, and I saw water levels going down," she said, "and I could see there was no longer firewood."

All of these were symptoms of desertification, which means that more and more land in Kenya was being taken over by desert. The northern part of the country had long been arid and inhospitable to growing crops, but now the infertile, desert-like conditions seemed to be expanding. Though the causes and processes of desertification are complex, one of the key factors is trees. Tree roots help bind the soil together and hold it in place. As trees are cut down for lumber and to create pastures and fields, the rich

77

topsoil can erode away. Also, the loss of shade dries out the soil and may even cause the climate to change, reducing the amount of rainfall.

There was a human side to this environmental issue. Like many former colonies in Africa, Kenya was a poor country where many people struggled to get by. The loss of trees and the expansion of the desert made the situation worse. The farmers' fields weren't as productive, so food became more scarce and more expensive. With fewer trees, firewood became harder to find. This had a big effect on people in rural areas, most of whom used wood fires to cook their meals. They began to eat more foods that didn't require cooking, and many of these items proved less nutritious than traditional cooked dishes. This contributed to the country's malnutrition problem.

> "The Green Belt Movement is about hope. It tells people that they are responsible for their own lives. It suggests that at the very least, you can plant a tree and improve your habitat. It raises an awareness that people can take control of their environment, which is the first step toward greater participation in society."

Maathai's personal life had an effect on her growing concern about the environment and poverty. In the late 1960s she married Mwangi Maathai, a business leader who had political aspirations. In 1974 her husband ran for a seat in Kenya's Parliament (similar to Congress in the United States), and Maathai accompanied him on the campaign trail. This gave her an even better look at the difficult lives of the country's underprivileged residents. "I had grown up in a poor rural area, but it was nothing like what I encountered in the slums of Nairobi," Maathai recalled. "These people were desperate. All they wanted was a promise from my husband that we would find them jobs. Of course he said he would, because that is what you say on a campaign. However, I took the promise very seriously."

Green Belt: Beginning a Movement

Faced by two large problems—a lack of trees and a lack of jobs—Maathai hit upon a solution that addressed both: pay people to plant trees. Her program was launched in 1977 under the direction of the National Council of Women of Kenya, a group that she had recently joined. The program was originally called Save the Land Harambee, using the Swahili term that

Wangari ready to plant a seedling for the Green Belt Movement.

means "let us all pull together." But the program later took on a new title: The Green Belt Movement, which also became the title of her book on the subject, *The Green Belt Movement: Sharing the Approach and the Experience*, first published in 1985 and reprinted in 2003. The program she developed provides free tree seedlings to the members of a community, who in most cases are women. The women plant the seedlings and care for them. For each tree that survives more than three months outside the nursery, the planter receives 50 Kenya cents (about 2.5 U.S. cents). This sounds like a very small amount of money, but one person can plant a lot of seedlings. Also, the income of poor Kenyans is so low that even a few dollars can make a huge difference in their lives.

A key to the success of the Green Belt Movement is that it is practical. As Maathai has noted, those struggling to make ends meet can't afford to volunteer their time for a cause that doesn't directly touch their lives. "Conservation cannot be presented to them as a luxury issue," she explained. "The trees have been planted to meet immediate community needs—to provide fuelwood and material for fencing and building, and to give shade." Early on, the organization received help from government nurseries that provided tree seedlings for free. The program grew quickly, however, and the demand became so great that the government had to start charging for the trees. Eventually, the organization established its own nursery in Nairobi, then encouraged women's groups around the country to do the same. By the late 1990s, 6,000 of these nurseries were in operation in Kenya.

Much of the group's funding comes from international organizations, but Green Belt relies on the knowledge and abilities of local people. The women use common-sense agricultural practices rather than complex scientific knowledge. These "foresters without diplomas," as Maathai calls them, were largely successful: about half of the trees planted in dry areas grew into adulthood, while about 8 of every 10 planted in wetter areas survived. By 1999, the movement had planted more than 20 million trees throughout Kenya and had employed about 50,000 people. The Green Belt program proved so successful, it spread to many other countries in Africa. In addition to planting trees, Green Belt also offers educational programs addressing civic affairs, the environment, health, nutrition, and other subjects. "The Green Belt Movement is about hope," Maathai said. "It tells people that they are responsible for their own lives. It suggests that at the very least, you can plant a tree and improve your habitat. It raises an awareness that people can take control of their environment, which is the first step toward greater participation in society."

> ———— " ————
>
> *"When you start working with the environment seriously,"* Maathai said, *"the whole arena comes: human rights, women's rights, environmental rights, children's rights, you know, everybody's rights."*
>
> ———— " ————

"Too Educated, Too Strong, Too Successful"

In addition to growing trees and putting people to work, Maathai began to focus on a variety of political issues. "When you start working with the environment seriously," she said, "the whole arena comes: human rights, women's rights, environmental rights, children's rights, you know, everybody's rights." Eventually, her concerns would make her an outspoken critic of her country's government, but first she had a personal matter to deal with.

In the early 1980s Maathai's husband filed for divorce, claiming that his wife had committed adultery with another member of Parliament. His case also asserted that she was "too educated, too strong, too successful, too stubborn, and too hard to control." She denied the adultery charge, and the case was settled in a well-publicized trial. When the court found in favor of her husband, Maathai charged that judges were either "incompetent or corrupt," which earned her a brief jail sentence for being in contempt of court. In the end, she believed that her marriage came to and end because her husband considered her a threat. "I think from his point of view I was a woman who was a little too, er . . . conspicuous for him," she said. "He was a politician and he wanted to be successful and I think I was a bit overshadowing to him, and I didn't realize."

Maathai didn't become any less conspicuous after the divorce. In 1982, her political activities forced her to give up her position at the University of Nairobi. According to one account of the incident, she decided to become a candidate for a Parliament seat and quit her job to concentrate on the campaign. She was later prevented from running because of a technicality, and the university refused to take her back. Maathai has charged that she was "forced out" of her job at the college. "The university told me I could either be an activist or an academic," she said, which eventually led to her resignation.

Fighting the Power

Maathai believes that "you cannot fight for the environment without eventually getting into conflict with the politicians." In fact, she came to believe that bad political leaders caused many of the problems facing her region of the world. "Some people believe that Africans live impoverished lives because they are unproductive and lack initiative," she wrote in *The Green Belt Movement,* "but nothing can be further from the truth. Much has to do with misgovernance by their leaders, and Africans have been poorly governed for a long time."

"A long time" describes the term of Kenya's president Daniel arap Moi, who took power after the death of Jomo Kenyatta in 1978 and remained there for the next 24 years. Moi's administration earned a reputation for corruption. For instance, government leaders were suspected of demanding payments, or "kickbacks," from contractors who wished to work for the government. Also, there is evidence that Moi personally amassed a fortune by misappropriating public money. Many Kenyans were opposed to his actions, but they had no effective way to remove him from office. The constitution prevented the establishment of any opposition political parties, so Moi and his KANU party faced no opposition in elections. Those who spoke out against this system were often arrested and tortured. Opposing President Moi could be very dangerous.

Yet that's the job Maathai took on in 1989. That year, Moi's party announced plans to build a 60-story skyscraper in the middle of Nairobi's Uhuru Park. Accompanied by a four-story-tall statue of Moi, the building

Maathai's work with the Green Belt Movement brought her in opposition to Danial arap Moi, President of Kenya from 1978 to 2002, whose administration was widely believed to be corrupt.

project would cost Kenya $200 million. In addition, the building's concrete and glass would take over a tree-filled park that was intended to be a refuge for the city's residents. "If I didn't react to their interfering with this park, I may as well not plant another tree," Maathai said. "I cannot condone that kind of activity and call myself an environmentalist." She filed a lawsuit in an attempt to stop the project and publicly denounced the government's priorities. "The people are starving. They need food; they need medicine; they need education. They do not need . . . a skyscraper to house the ruling party and a 24-hour TV station."

Moi and his cronies struck back at Maathai. The president called her "a mad woman" who was "a threat to the order and security of the country," and she was publicly denounced in Kenya's Parliament. Many politicians brought up the issue of her divorce, saying that she was inspired by a hatred of men. Maathai wasn't intimidated, and she continued to speak out against the building. "They think they can embarrass and silence me with threats and name-calling," she said. "But I have an elephant's skin." She lost her legal challenge, but the controversy she created about the tower gave the project's financial backers second thoughts. In the end, the president's skyscraper was never built.

Suffering for Her Actions

Maathai learned that name-calling wasn't the only weapon that could be used against her. The Green Belt Movement was suddenly evicted from the government-owned building where it had its offices. As a result, the group was forced to operate out of Maathai's home for a time. The group's tree-planting work was also interfered with. Still, she was committed to being an outspoken activist. "I may get into serious trouble," she admitted. "They may physically abuse me. . . . But every time you provide leadership — every time you speak out, you expect you may suffer for what you believe in."

Her prediction of physical abuse soon came true. In March 1992, Maathai participated in a hunger strike seeking freedom for political prisoners in Kenya. Riot police attacked the peaceful gathering, and she was clubbed unconscious. She was arrested on numerous occasions but was aided by supporters outside Kenya who pressured the authorities to set her free. In 1993, she tried to stop ethnic violence in Kenya's Rift Valley. Disagreements there between different cultural groups had resulted in more than 1,000 deaths. Maathai charged that Moi's government was inciting the violence so that the president's group (the Kalenjin) could drive out their rivals. She founded the Tribal Clashes Resettlement Volunteer Service to assist those displaced by violence.

> "I may get into serious trouble," Maathai admitted. "They may physically abuse me. . . . But every time you provide leadership — every time you speak out, you expect you may suffer for what you believe in."

Though Maathai and other protestors faced many difficulties and dangers, they began to have an effect on the Kenyan political system. President Moi felt the pressure of growing resistance within the country as well as complaints by international governments and organizations. In 1991, the ban on opposition political parties was lifted, allowing greater political freedom. A year later, the first multiparty elections in decades took place, though Moi was once again elected president and his KANU party remained in power. Maathai's supporters urged her to run for office, but she refused for several years. Then, in 1997, she not only ran for a seat in Parliament but also for president. Her campaign as candidate for the Liberal Party of Kenya (LPK) didn't fare well, however. She entered the race late, just a month before the election. Then, on the day before the voting, a rumor circulated that she had withdrawn from the election, though Maathai later claimed this was untrue. According to some accounts, her party deserted her at the last moment. Whatever the cause, she received little support and wasn't elected to either office. Instead President Moi was returned to yet another term.

Defending the Forest

The following year, Maathai returned to a more familiar role — defending one of Kenya's nature areas. The Karura National Forest, near Nairobi, had been established to protect one of the last patches of virgin forest in Kenya. But in 1998 President Moi's government sold one-third of it to developers who wanted to build a luxury housing development. Maathai and other protestors objected to the sale, but that didn't stop developers from beginning to fell trees. The situation became more tense after equipment belonging to the developers was set on fire. Then, in December 1998 and January 1999, violence erupted in a series of confrontations between protestors and private security guards who had been hired by the developers. While Maathai and her colleagues tried to carry out a demonstration, 200 men armed with clubs and whips attacked them. Maathai suffered a blow to the head and dropped to her knees, blood pouring from a scalp wound. Her friends pulled her out of the melee and drove her to a police station. She filed a complaint saying that she had been assaulted, then signed the form in her own blood. From her hospital room she vowed that "as soon as I recover, I shall return to Karura forest, even if they bury me there."

The controversy over Karura soon grew larger. Prominent religious leaders in Kenya sided with the environmentalists, as did students from the University of Nairobi. In late January 1999, the student protests turned into riots in the streets of the capital. These protests created more negative publicity about the housing development at Karura, and the project was finally abandoned. "We stopped them," Maathai said, but she soon had to take up similar battles in other parts of Kenya. In the early 2000s, the government attempted to give away more public lands, with Maathai and her colleagues fighting them every step of the way.

Winning the Vote

As the 2002 elections approached, many Kenyans wondered if their country was finally about to see an important political change. Thanks to a law passed in 1992, President Moi was prevented from seeking another term in office. He was still very powerful, however, and hoped to see his hand-picked successor become president. Kenya's opposition parties united

After private developers began felling trees in Karura National Forest, a peaceful demonstration turned violent when hired security guards attacked demonstrators. ABOVE: Maathai and others argue with security guards at Karura Forest. BELOW: Maathai was hospitalized after she was injured in the demonstration at Karura Forest.

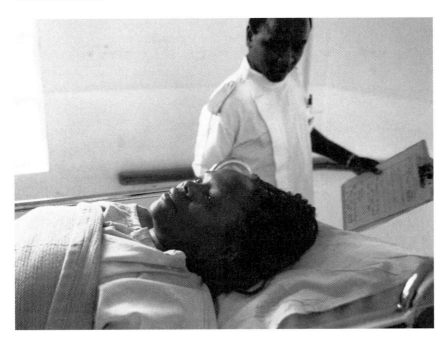

against Moi, forming the National Rainbow Coalition (NARC) with Mwai Kibaki as their presidential candidate. Maathai joined the NARC coalition and once again ran for a seat in Parliament. On election day, NARC swept to victory. Kibaki became Kenya's president, and Maathai became one of the country's lawmakers. Upon taking office, Kibaki gave Maathai an additional responsibility by appointing her Assistant Minister for the Environment in charge of natural resources and wildlife.

"I'm very excited," Maathai said of her new role in government. "For me it is the next step and a very, very important step. I sit in Parliament sometimes and remind myself, 'you're really making laws here.' If a law is made then you actually have an opportunity to influence future generations." At the same time, she came to understand that being a part of government can be as difficult as opposing it. "It's a very slow process," she said. "I try to be persuasive, but [things are] not moving as fast as I would have liked." As usual, she emphasized measures related to the country's trees in her parliamentary work. For instance, she sought funding to purchase seedlings and promoted the establishment of a national tree-planting day.

While her governmental duties keep her busy, Maathai has continued to express her opinions on a range of important topics. Her attitude toward HIV-AIDS has created controversy. *The Standard*, a Kenyan newspaper, quoted her as saying "AIDS is not a curse from God to Africans or the black people. It is a tool to control them designed by some evil-minded scientists." The quote seemed to suggest that Maathai believed AIDS had been purposely invented to harm blacks. She later distanced herself from this view. In an essay entitled "The Challenge of AIDS in Africa" published on her web site, Maathai wrote that "I neither say nor believe that the virus was developed by white people or white powers in order to destroy the African people. Such views are wicked and destructive."

Winning the Nobel Peace Prize

Over the years, Maathai has accepted many awards from international agencies. She's become somewhat accustomed to receiving the news of such prizes, but in October 2004, she got an exciting phone call: The Norwegian ambassador to Kenya notified her that she had just won the Nobel Peace Prize. The Nobel Prizes are some of the most prestigious honors in the world and are given out annually by the Nobel Foundation, which is based in Norway and Sweden. The awards cover several different fields, with the Peace Prize going to the person or group whose actions have promoted world peace. In announcing the award, the Nobel Committee stated that "Maathai stands at the front of the fight to promote ecologically viable

Maathai with her Nobel Peace Prize and certificate.

social, economic, and cultural development in Kenya and in Africa." She was the first African woman and the first environmentalist to win the prize.

"I am absolutely overwhelmed," Maathai said after getting the news. "This is the biggest surprise in my entire life." In addition to the worldwide fame that comes with the award, she received $1.36 million U.S. "That's a lot of money," she said. "I've not had so much money in my life. It's so much I don't know what I'll be able to do with it. But I do know it will go to improve the work we do."

———— " ————

"Some people have asked what the relationship is between peace and environment, and to them I say that many wars are fought over resources, which are becoming increasingly scarce across the earth. If we did a better job of managing our resources sustainably, conflicts over them would be reduced. So, protecting the global environment is directly related to securing peace.... When we plant trees, we plant the seeds of peace and seeds of hope."

———— " ————

Maathai was something of a surprise choice for the Nobel Peace Prize, and some commentators wondered why the prize went to someone best known for environmental work. When she publicly accepted the award, she addressed this subject: "Some people have asked what the relationship is between peace and environment, and to them I say that many wars are fought over resources, which are becoming increasingly scarce across the earth. If we did a better job of managing our resources sustainably, conflicts over them would be reduced. So, protecting the global environment is directly related to securing peace.... When we plant trees, we plant the seeds of peace and seeds of hope."

MARRIAGE AND FAMILY

Maathai married Mwangi Maathai in the late 1960s, and they were divorced in the early 1980s. The couple had three children, Waweru, Wanjira, and Muta, who were primarily raised by their mother. During the years when Maathai's activism earned her powerful enemies, she sent her children to the United States. She felt they would be safer there and could pursue their educations in American schools, just as she had done. In fact, her son Waweru attended the same college in Atchison, Kansas, that his mother attended (it's now known as Benedictine College). Maathai divides her time between Nairobi, her primary home since the mid-1960s, and the Tetu constituency that she represents in Parliament. That area is located near Mt. Kenya, the country's highest mountain, and includes Nyeri, the town where Maathai was born.

SELECTED WRITINGS

The Green Belt Movement: Sharing the Approach and the Experience, 1985; reprinted 2003

HONORS AND AWARDS

Woman of the Year Award: 1983
Right Livelihood Award: 1984
Award for the Protection of the Global Environment (Better World
    Society): 1986
Windstar Award for the Environment: 1988
Woman of the World Award: 1989
Offeramus Medal: 1990
Africa Prize for Leadership (The Hunger Project): 1991
Goldman Environmental Prize: 1991
Edinburgh Medal: 1993
Jane Addams Women's Leadership Award: 1993
Golden Ark Award: 1994
Member, International Women's Hall of Fame: 1995
Hero of the Planet Award (*Time* magazine): 1998
Juliette Hollister Award: 2001
Montgomery Fellow (Dartmouth College): 2001
McCluskey Visiting Fellow in Conservation (Global Institute for
    Sustainable Forestry, Yale University): 2002
Outstanding Vision and Commitment Award (Bridges to Community): 2002
WANGO Environment Award: 2003
Arbor Day Award: 2004
Conservation Scientist Award (Center for Environmental Research and
    Conservation): 2004
Elder of the Burning Spear citation (Republic of Kenya): 2004
J. Sterling Morton Award: 2004
Petra Kelly Prize for the Environment: 2004
Sophie Prize: 2004
Nobel Peace Prize: 2004
100 Heroes and Icons (*Time* magazine): 2005

FURTHER READING

Books

Biography Today World Leaders Series, Vol. 1: *Environmental Leaders*, 1997
Contemporary Authors, Vol. 155, 1997
Contemporary Black Biography, Vol. 43, 2004
Maathai, Wangari. *The Green Belt Movement: Sharing the Approach and the
    Experience*, 1985; reprinted 2003
Notable Scientists: From 1900 to the Present, 2001
Who's Who in the World, 2005

Periodicals

Chicago Tribune, May 22, 2005, p.C4
Current Biography Yearbook, 1993
Ebony, Mar. 2005, p.22
Financial Times (London), Nov. 5, 1994, p.26; Mar. 12, 2005, p.3
In Context: A Quarterly of Humane Sustainable Culture, Spring 1991, p.55
Independent Sunday (London), Feb. 7, 1999, p.18
Los Angeles Times, Oct. 9, 2004, p.A1; Oct. 17, 2004, p.M6
New Internationalist, July 2004, p.33
New Scientist, July 22, 2000, p.42
New York Times, Dec. 6, 1989, p.A4; Oct. 9, 2004, pp.A1 and A7; Dec. 10, 2004, p.41
O Magazine, June 2005, p.71
People, Oct. 9, 2004, p.71
Time, Apr. 18, 2005, p.98
U.S. News & World Report, Jan. 10, 2005, p.56
Washington Post, June 2, 1992, p.D1; Dec. 26, 2004, p.D1
World Watch, May-June 2004, p.26

Online Databases

Biography Resource Center Online, 2005, articles from *African Biography,* 1999; *Contemporary Authors Online,* 2004; *Contemporary Black Biography,* 2004; and *Notable Scientists: From 1900 to the Present,* 2001

ADDRESS

Wangari Maathai
The Green Belt Movement
P.O. Box 67545
Nairobi, Kenya

WORLD WIDE WEB SITES

http://www.wangarimaathai.or.ke
http://www.greenbeltmovement.org
http://nobelprize.org/peace/laureates/2004/index.html
http://www.goldmanprize.org/recipients/recipients.html

Violet Palmer 1964-

American Professional Basketball Referee
First Woman to Officiate an NBA Game

BIRTH

Violet Palmer was born in 1964 in Compton, a tough section of Los Angeles, California. Her father, James Palmer, was a metalworker in a factory that made airplane parts. Her mother, Gussie Palmer, was a homemaker. Violet was the second of four children in her family. She has two sisters — one older and one younger — as well as a younger brother.

YOUTH

Throughout her youth, Violet enjoyed the stability and support of a close-knit family. Her parents provided for all her needs and always encouraged her to pursue her dreams. She acknowledged that "My friends say, 'Violet, you grew up in Compton, but your family was like *Little House on the Prairie*,'" referring to the book series by Laura Ingalls Wilder that was made into a popular TV show. "It's true. As a child, I never wanted for anything. I think a lot of my confidence and stability comes from my strong family background."

When Violet was about 10 years old, her father put up a basketball hoop in the backyard. She spent hours playing basketball with her brother and the neighborhood boys. "The guys knew that she could play," said her brother, Rod. "She was one of the first to be picked all the time."

EDUCATION

Palmer attended Compton High School, where she became a star athlete. She played softball, ran track, and was the starting point guard for the girls' basketball team. After graduating from high school, she went on to attend California State Polytechnic University at Pomona (Cal Poly-Pomona). She served as captain of the women's basketball team for three years, leading Cal Poly-Pomona to back-to-back NCAA Division II national championships in 1985 and 1986. Palmer earned a bachelor of science (BS) degree, with a major in recreation management and a minor in public administration, in 1987.

CAREER HIGHLIGHTS

Becoming a Referee

At the time Palmer completed her college basketball career, there were no professional basketball leagues for women in the United States. She was not interested in playing in Europe, but she wanted to remain involved in basketball in some capacity. She tried coaching high school basketball, but she only lasted one season. "The kids needed so much attention," she remembered. "I had migraines. I was just so tense and stressed out. I said, 'This ain't for me.'"

Palmer then took a job with the Placentia Recreation Department, near Los Angeles. Part of her job involved refereeing youth basketball leagues. She soon found that she enjoyed working as a basketball official. Her college basketball coach, Darlene May, encouraged her to pursue a career as a referee. May was a top women's basketball referee who became the first woman to officiate a women's basketball game in the Olympics.

Palmer soon began refereeing high school basketball games, and she was selected to officiate the Los Angeles city semifinals in her first year. She quickly moved up to the college level, refereeing women's basketball games in the Big West, West Coast, and PAC-10 conferences. "After just one year of officiating high school, I'm hired to do three college conferences. Unheard of," she stated. "I think my quick rise can be attributed to being an ex-player. I caught on extremely quickly."

Palmer studied basketball rules and regulations and attended special referee training camps during the summers. After impressing observers at summer camps in 1992, she received a schedule that included 40 NCAA

Palmer (#12) battling for the ball in 1985, while playing for Cal Poly-Pomona. The team won the first of the school's five NCAA Division II national championships.

Division I women's basketball games. Unfortunately, her career suffered a setback when she tore ligaments in her knee during a coed softball game. "Guy slides into first, clips me. Blows out my knee," she recalled. "I ended up in a cast from the top of my leg right down to my foot. Out for the year."

At first, Palmer worried that missing a year of refereeing might halt her career progress. "Until my injury, I didn't realize how important officiating was to me," she noted. "How much I really wanted to do it. That year I made a commitment to myself." Luckily, the college conferences recognized her abilities and held her spot until she recovered. "She had an extraordinary amount of talent, terrific personality and communication skills," said PAC-10 officiating supervisor Carter Rankin. "She also had the greatest asset any official can have: anticipatory movement." In 1993 Palmer officiated 50 Division I women's basketball games. The following year she was honored to have the opportunity to referee a Final Four game in the NCAA tournament.

Training for the NBA

By 1995 Palmer was thrilled with the progress she had made in her career as a referee. In the five years since she had officiated her first game, she had rocketed to the highest levels of women's basketball. Since there were no female referees in men's college or professional basketball, however, she thought that perhaps she had advanced as far as possible.

Then, to her surprise, Palmer received a call from Aaron Wade, who was in charge of developing officials for the National Basketball Association (NBA). Wade told her that the league was hoping to develop some female referees and invited her to attend a training camp. Palmer was one of two women to attend the camp, along with Dee Kantner. She immediately found that she had to make some adjustments, since the NBA players were bigger, faster, and stronger than the players she usually officiated. "I had to become a student again," she recalled. "I was learning where to be, where to look. That's when the training came in. If you learn the mechanics, you become a better referee, instantly."

> "I had to become a student again," Palmer said about starting to work in the NBA, where the players were bigger, faster, and stronger than the players she usually officiated. "I was learning where to be, where to look. That's when the training came in. If you learn the mechanics, you become a better referee, instantly."

Palmer was invited back to the NBA's training camp for new referees in 1996. Her performance got the attention of Rod Thorn, the vice president of operations for the NBA, who invited her to participate in another training camp that featured veteran NBA officials. As part of this experience, Palmer was assigned to referee an NBA exhibition game. Up to this point, Palmer had viewed the NBA training as a useful tool that would increase her skills for refereeing women's basketball. It was only after she officiated an exhibition game that she thought she might have a chance to become an NBA referee. "A lightbulb went off in my head," she remembered. "I said to myself, 'You're gonna do this. You're gonna show everybody that thought this was impossible that it is possible.' I wasn't scared—I knew I could do it. I had been an athlete all my life and knew I just needed the training. But I was totally nervous. I couldn't believe it was happening, but that's a normal feeling."

In the meantime, Palmer continued to perform well as a women's college basketball referee. She had a great season in 1996-97, which culminated in her having the opportunity to officiate the NCAA women's basketball national championship game between Old Dominion and Tennessee. That summer Palmer attended the veterans' camp again and officiated five NBA exhibition games. Afterward, Thorn hired her to join the 58-person officiating staff for the NBA. Along with Kantner, who was hired at the same time, Palmer became one of the first female referees in the NBA. "We look for the best possible refs," Thorn explained. "Violet Palmer has an on-court presence. She's a tough, no-nonsense person with excellent referee skills."

Making History

Palmer made history on October 31, 1997, when she took the court to refer-ee an NBA game between the Vancouver Grizzlies and the Dallas Mavericks. She not only became the first female referee in the history of the league, but also the first woman to officiate any major American men's pro-fessional sporting event (Kantner took the court for the first time a few days later). "I will never, ever forget the moment I put that jacket on and walked onto that floor," she said. "It was like, 'Wow, you're telling me I'm going to do this every night!' I was more than nervous, I was going to pee in my pants."

That night, Palmer was part of a three-person officiating crew that includ-ed veterans Billy Oakes and Mark Wunderlich. All NBA officiating crews consist of three people. The least experienced official is the umpire, the second official is the referee, and the most experienced official is the crew chief. All three officials are allowed to make calls, but the crew chief gener-ally sets the tone for the game and takes responsibility for resolving dis-putes about rules or the time clock.

The other members of Palmer's first officiating crew recognized the impor-tance of the occasion. In fact, Oakes placed a photo of himself and Palmer on the court in Vancouver in the scrapbook of his career. "I know you cher-ish that first night," he told her later, "but you would not believe how proud I was to be part of it with you." Thorn made a point of attending Palmer's debut game. Afterward, he praised her performance under pres-sure. "She did her job, like the other two officials on the court," he stated. "The better she performs, the more anonymous she'll become."

Palmer in action in her first game as an NBA referee,
in Vancouver, Canada, October 1997.

Over the first few months of the 1997-98 NBA season, Palmer and Kantner received a great deal of media attention. The introduction of female referees generated some negative reaction around the league—from fans, coaches, and players. For example, the outspoken player Charles Barkley declared that it was a man's game and should only involve men. Other NBA stars questioned whether female referees could keep up with the fast pace of the men's game, or expressed concerns about swearing in front of a woman on the court. But Palmer took it all in stride and tried to do her job. "There are a couple of players saying negative things but that's the way it goes," she noted. "You're always going to have one or two players like that. But most players, I don't think they care who you are. They just want good referees."

A number of other players expressed their support for the addition of female officials to the NBA. "I'm all for it," said Denver Nuggets guard Kenny Smith. "Women have better judgment than men." Chris Mullin of the Indiana Pacers gave Palmer and Kantner a compliment by saying that they were no different than their male counterparts. "They've done a fine job," he stated. "We've had them both for games, but I can't even remember which games. Nothing sticks out."

From the beginning, Palmer was gratified by the reception she received from her fellow referees. "All the referees were supportive. They were unbelievably open and treated me like one of the guys," she noted. "The bottom line is not that I'm a woman but what happens in between that 94 feet [the length of the basketball court]. There are three referees on the court and they're the only friends you have down there. So they can't look at me and say 'I don't want to work with her.' You just can't do that. The players don't care. The coaches don't care. They just want the calls to be fair. They won't say a woman screwed up, they'll say the ref screwed up. And we do mess up. We're human."

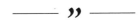

> *The introduction of female referees generated some negative reaction, but Palmer took it all in stride. "There are a couple of players saying negative things but that's the way it goes. You're always going to have one or two players like that. But most players, I don't think they care who you are. They just want good referees."*

Gaining Respect

Palmer has continued to progress as a referee since her rookie season. Now an eight-year veteran NBA official, she still finds her job exciting, although she admits that the constant traveling can be tough. Like most other referees in the league, Palmer works from late September through late April each year. She officiates between 11 and 13 games per month, or about 75 games per season. For each game, she must travel to the home team's city and arrive at the arena three hours early to prepare. Palmer and her officiating crew study the teams and players that will be involved in each game. They need to know the disruptive personalities on every team, how long the visiting team has been on the road, both teams' record in recent games, and any personnel changes or controversies. After a game ends, Palmer typically spends another hour or two watching film in the locker room with the other members of the officiating crew to evaluate their performance. She also takes weekly quizzes and video tests to make sure she remains current on the rules.

—————— 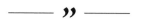 ——————

When asked what factors most contributed to her success as an NBA referee, Palmer responded: "Presence. I think I have that on the court. I know I do. I've never been a follower. I've always been a leader. I feel I have total control out there. I am in charge. I can handle anything."

—————— " ——————

NBA referees are required to know the rule book inside and out, remain in top physical condition, and undergo a health examination annually. They also must be mentally tough. "This is a tough profession because you're always being scrutinized," Palmer conceded. "If you're a ref, you're going to be booed and yelled at and worse—it has nothing to do with being male or female."

When asked what factors most contributed to her success as an NBA referee, Palmer responded: "Presence. I think I have that on the court. I know I do. I've never been a follower. I've always been a leader. I feel I have total control out there. I am in charge. I can handle anything." In contrast, the NBA's other female referee, Dee Kantner, was fired in 2002. She was the lowest-ranked official among coaches and general managers, largely because she lacked the on-court presence needed to maintain her authority among the best players in the world. Kantner later became the supervisor of officials in the WNBA.

Some observers claim that, as an African-American woman in her 40s, Palmer has a unique advantage in gaining the respect of players. Since many of the NBA's young stars were raised by single mothers, they tend to view her as an authority figure. "She almost looks like your mother," said Golden State Warriors forward Danny Fortson. "She gives you that look

Being an NBA referee requires a certain forcefulness on the court, as in this episode where Palmer ejected Miami Heat player Alonzo Mourning (center) from the court, while Coach Pat Riley (right) looked on.

like, 'Shut your mouth!' I got that look from my mom. I know what that look means." "No question they see her in a different light," said veteran NBA official Nolan Fine. "You can see it in the players' body language." Palmer says that she will accept any source of respect from NBA players. "Everybody has advantages and everybody in this job has to use them," she noted. "I hear guys say, 'We're not messing with that sister right now, she's got that look.' I like that. I'll take it."

Palmer hopes that the next step in her career will be making the 32-person crew that is chosen to referee the NBA playoffs. Since it usually takes between 8 and 10 years of experience before officials are selected to the playoff crew, she appears to be right on track. "I'm not reffing playoff games yet but I'm looking forward to it. I'm just waiting my turn. And it's coming, too. The door will open again and I'm gonna put my foot right in," she stated. "That would be like the pot of gold at the end of the rainbow."

Palmer also hopes that the day will soon come when she is no longer viewed as a *female* referee. "I'm very proud to be a woman referee, don't get me wrong," she said. "But I am not on some woman kick or anything like that. The recognition I want is to be accepted as a good referee." She hopes to keep working in the NBA for another 15 or 20 years. "I have a great life," she noted. "I love what I do. I can't believe they actually pay me to do it. It's like a dream come true. I feel truly blessed."

HOME AND FAMILY

Palmer, who is single, lives in Carson, California, with her shih tzu dog, Mozhi.

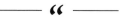

"I have a great life. I love what I do. I can't believe they actually pay me to do it. It's like a dream come true. I feel truly blessed."

HOBBIES AND OTHER INTERESTS

In her spare time, Palmer enjoys playing golf. She also likes helping young people who aspire to be referees. She spends a good part of each summer teaching at referee camps, and she also makes frequent visits to schools for career days. "I have the opportunity to make a difference," she explained. "I can tell kids the world offers so much—that if they get out there, those doors will open for them. I was working with the city and was happy, but look what happened. I'm at the top of the pedestal for refereeing. You can't get any higher than what I am. I'm blessed and very fortunate."

HONORS AND AWARDS

Top 10 Women Role Models (Ms. Foundation): 1997

FURTHER READING

Books

Notable Black American Women, 2002
Who's Who among African Americans, 2004

Periodicals

Chicago Sun-Times, Apr. 19, 1998, Sports, p.13
Dallas Morning News, Nov. 2, 1997, p.A1
Denver Post, Oct. 21, 1997, p.D12
Ebony, Feb. 1998, p.172

ESPN Magazine, Mar. 4, 2003, p.44
Essence, Aug. 1998, p.60; Nov. 2004, p.42
LA Weekly, Aug. 1, 1997, p.57
Los Angeles Times, Oct. 29, 1997, p.A1; Oct. 30, 1997, p.C6
Newsweek, Mar. 8, 2004, p.38
People, Nov. 17, 1997, p.235
Philadelphia Tribune, June 19, 2001, p.D1
Seattle Times, Apr. 30, 2000, p.D1
Sports Illustrated, Nov. 10, 1997, p.30

Online Articles

http://sportsillustrated.cnn.com
   (*Sports Illustrated*/CNN, "Women of the Court," May 1, 1999)
http://www.referee.com
   (*Referee Magazine,* "Ultra Violet," Jan. 2000)
http://espn.go.com/nba/columns
   (ESPN, "The Truth about Refereeing in the NBA," Feb. 24, 2003)

Online Databases

Biography Resource Center Online, 2005, articles from *Notable Black American Women,* 2002, and *Who's Who among African Americans,* 2004

ADDRESS

Violet Palmer
NBA
645 5th Avenue
Olympic Tower, 10th Floor
New York, NY 10022

WORLD WIDE WEB SITE

http://www.referee.com

Carlos Santana 1947-

Mexican-Born American Guitarist and Band Leader
Winner of Eight Grammy Awards for His Album
Supernatural

BIRTH

Carlos Santana was born on July 20, 1947, in Autlan de Navarro, a small town in the state of Jalisco in west-central Mexico.
His father, Jose Santana, was a violin player in a traditional
Mexican mariachi band. His mother, Josefina (Barragan) Santana, was a homemaker. Carlos is the fourth-oldest among
the seven children in his family. He has two brothers and four
sisters.

YOUTH

Carlos grew up in a close-knit, religious family. "From my mother, I learned that everything in life is borrowed from the Lord," he recalled. "From my father, I learned that life is service. From both parents, I learned good manners." Like their neighbors in Autlan de Navarro, the Santanas lived in a modest house that did not have electricity or running water. All of the children were expected to help out with the chores and share clothing and other belongings.

Carlos developed a passion for music at an early age. Realizing that music had the power to make people happy, he longed to become a musician himself. "As a kid, I remember watching how people's eyes would light up when my father played his violin," he noted. "I read books about how people in their 30s or 40s are just beginning to find out what their purpose in life is. I found that out when I was five years old." At that time his father started teaching him to play the violin. But Carlos disliked the instrument and grew frustrated at his inability to master it. "My father's a musician, his father was a musician, my great-grandfather was a musician. Dad taught me the violin for almost seven years, and I could never get anything out of it," he remembered. "I just couldn't get a feeling for it. My playing was no good."

> —— " ——
>
> *"As a kid, I remember watching how people's eyes would light up when my father played his violin. I read books about how people in their 30s or 40s are just beginning to find out what their purpose in life is. I found that out when I was five years old."*
>
> —— " ——

Jose Santana traveled all over Mexico and California with his band, sometimes leaving home for months at a time. During a particularly long absence in the mid-1950s, Josefina Santana grew concerned that her husband might never return. So in 1955, when Carlos was eight years old, his mother packed up the children and moved north to Tijuana, a town along the U.S. border, to look for Jose. Luckily, they were soon able to find him.

Carlos and his family spent the next five years living in Tijuana—a bustling town full of shops, bars, and restaurants, as well as beggars and prostitutes. During this time, Carlos gained his first exposure to American music. He felt an immediate connection with the blues and early rock and roll played by such artists as B.B. King and John Lee Hooker. As a result, he soon rejected the traditional Mexican folk music favored by his father. "Blues was my first love," he explained. "It was the first thing where I said, 'Oh man, this is the stuff.' It just sounded so raw and honest, gut-bucket honest. From then I started rebelling." He stopped playing violin and instead took up the guitar. Playing on the streets of Tijuana in order to collect change from passing tourists, he soon graduated to playing in local bands. By the age of 11, he was appearing regularly in Tijuana nightclubs and earning enough money to help support his family.

In 1960, when Carlos was 13, his family immigrated to the United States. They settled among the large Mexican population in the Mission District of San Francisco, California. At first Carlos felt out of place in San Francisco. Since he did not speak English and had already supported himself by playing guitar in Tijuana nightclubs, he felt that he had little in common with American kids his age. His unhappiness with the new living situation caused him to act out against his parents—arguing, skipping school, and refusing to eat. Finally, in desperation, his mother gave him $20 and sent him back to Tijuana to try to make it on his own.

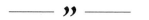

> "Blues was my first love. It was the first thing where I said, 'Oh man, this is the stuff.' It just sounded so raw and honest, gut-bucket honest. From then I started rebelling."

Carlos lived alone in Tijuana for nearly a year, and it was a difficult time for him. Years later, he revealed that he had suffered sexual abuse during this period. But he also continued his musical education and became an accomplished guitar player. In 1962 his family convinced him to return to the United States. This time he found a reason to stay. At that time, an alternative culture was just starting to develop in San Francisco, and it included a diverse array of musical styles—including jazz, blues, folk, and salsa. "The '60s was the most important decade of the century," he stated. "To me, the [San Francisco] Bay Area was supremely important in creating a whole new frequency for the rest of the world. I was very fortunate to be here at that time."

EDUCATION

During his early years in Tijuana, Santana attended a Catholic elementary school. He often complained to his parents that the teachers there were mean, always yelling at or hitting the students. When his family first moved to San Francisco, Santana attended James Lick Junior High School.

"It was a drag," he noted. "They put me back into junior high because I couldn't speak English. I had to adapt to a whole other way of thinking and being around kids, because I thought I was a man of the world after playing in this nightclub in Tijuana and watching ladies strip. To me, I was a grown-up, but when I came here, I had to live the life of an adolescent all over again, and I couldn't relate."

Santana's troubles in school contributed to his desire to move back to Tijuana. Upon his return to the U.S. in 1962, he attended Mission High School in San Francisco. By this time his sole focus was music, and he showed little interest in his studies. "I would only show up in the morning for homeroom. They would take attendance and then I would split," he admitted. "I didn't want to know about algebra or George Washington or whatever. I could hardly wait to get out of school." Nevertheless, Santana somehow managed to graduate in 1965. "They were very gracious to give me my diploma," he acknowledged.

CAREER HIGHLIGHTS

Appearing at Woodstock

Throughout high school, Santana had told anyone who would listen that he planned to become a professional musician and play with great artists. "People would ask, 'What are you going to do when you leave school?'" he recalled. "I'd say, 'I'm going to play with Michael Bloomfield and B.B. King.' They'd say, 'Man, you're tripping.'" After graduation, Santana worked as a dishwasher in a restaurant and played music on the streets of San Francisco for change. As he improved he began joining jam sessions with a variety of musicians and bands. In 1966 he formed his own band with some of these musicians: David Brown on bass; Gregg Rolie on keyboards and vocals; Rod Harper on drums; and Tom Frazer on guitar. Originally known as the Santana Blues Band, the group soon changed its name to Santana. "The reason we chose my name was because it sounded the best," Carlos Santana explained. "Santana was something that could be a galaxy. It could be a planet or it could be the winds. It had a universal resonance to it." The name also proved appropriate for the group, however, because Carlos Santana's soaring guitar solos provided its trademark sound.

Santana started out playing in small clubs in San Francisco. Over the next three years, the band added more Latin rhythms to its sound and rose to regional fame. "We started mixing up jazz and blues, and some African flavor," Carlos Santana recalled. "We had something different than what was being played in San Francisco." In 1968 Santana played a historic series of concerts at San Francisco's Fillmore West Auditorium, a legendary concert

Part of the original poster for Santana's 1968 Live at the Fillmore concerts.

hall. (Thirty years later, the group released a two-CD set called *Live at the Fillmore* featuring songs recorded during these performances.) These shows helped Santana gain a reputation as an exciting and innovative live band. Also in 1968, the group appeared alongside such notable acts as the Grateful Dead and Muddy Waters at the Sky River Rock Festival in Washington State.

By early 1969, Santana had undergone the first in a long string of person-nel changes. Original members Frazer and Harper left the band, while drummer Michael Shrieve and percussionists Mike Carabello and Jose Chepito Areas joined it. This incarnation of Santana made a triumphant appearance at the legendary Woodstock Festival in New York during the summer of 1969. Playing in front of an audience of half a million people,

Santana showcased its unusual fusion of Latin rhythms and rock guitar. The highlight of the band's set was the rock anthem "Soul Sacrifice," which was written specifically for Woodstock. This song was featured in a famous 1970 film about the weekend-long concert event.

Although some people criticized Woodstock as a bad cultural influence — citing drug use and lewd behavior among both performers and audience members — Carlos Santana remembered it fondly. "Some people called it a disaster area, but I didn't see nobody in a state of disaster," he stated. "I saw a lot of people coming together, sharing, and having a great time. If that was out of control, then America needs to lose control at least once a week."

Releasing Hit Records

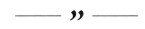

Santana's success at Woodstock brought the band a great deal of attention. Within a few weeks, the group appeared on the "Ed Sullivan Show" and signed a recording contract with Columbia Records. In October 1969 Santana released its debut album, entitled *Santana*. The album featured the hit single "Evil Ways," as well as the songs "Soul Sacrifice" and "Jingo." It was a phenomenal success, spending two years on the pop charts and selling over two million copies.

"When I was in high school, there were certain songs, like 'Louie Louie,' 'Gloria,' or 'Satisfaction,' that made everybody go crazy. The first time I heard 'Oye Como Va,' I knew it was a serious 'party forever' song. And since then, it's like a feeding frenzy every time we play it."

Santana released its second album, *Abraxas*, in 1970. Widely considered a classic, the band's follow-up effort featured the hit songs "Black Magic Woman" and "Oye Como Va." The latter became a signature song for the band's concert performances. "When I was in high school, there were certain songs, like 'Louie Louie,' 'Gloria,' or 'Satisfaction,' that made everybody go crazy," he noted. "The first time I heard 'Oye Como Va,' I knew it was a serious 'party forever' song. And since then, it's like a feeding frenzy every time we play it." *Abraxas* eventually sold four million copies.

In 1971 Santana released its third album, *Santana III*, which featured the hit song "Everything's Coming Our Way" and sold over one million copies. Around this time, however, the band essentially broke up. Although the members continued to record together on occasion, they no longer performed in concert. Some observers attributed the demise of this early—

Abraxas.

and hugely successful—version of the band to the influence of drugs. Others blamed Carlos Santana's newfound interest in jazz, which the other band members did not share. In any case, the band's first three albums were considered so seminal that they were all re-released in 1998.

Going Solo

Carlos Santana retained the legal rights to the name "Santana," and he continued to use it for bands featuring different collections of musicians over the years. But he also launched a solo career at this time. He recorded a live album with drummer Buddy Miles in 1972, for example, and made guest appearances on albums by such rock and jazz artists as Jefferson Airplane, Alice Coltrane, John McLaughlin, and Herbie Hancock. Although Carlos Santana was best known for his Latin-inspired rock guitar work, he began moving toward a more improvisational jazz fusion sound at this time.

Around 1973, following the drug-related deaths of several prominent musicians, Santana reassessed his lifestyle. His search for spiritual growth led him to become a disciple of the Bhakti Yoga guru Sri Chinmoy. He adopted the name Devadip Carlos Santana during the decade he spent as a follower of Chinmoy. "My time with Sri Chinmoy . . . gave me some discipline and an awareness of Eastern philosophy," Santana explained. "But I look at it like my old tennis shoes from Mission High School. They don't fit me anymore." Santana also met and married Deborah King during this time, and they eventually had three children together.

Santana maintained an active musical career throughout the 1970s and into the 1980s, both solo and with a band. Although none of the albums he released during this time approached the impact of his first three, his live performances continued to attract large crowds. "Mr. Santana's shows can be extraordinary—a fusion of rock, Latin music, and jazz—and they brim with his own improvising," music critic Peter Watrous wrote in the *New York Times.* "It's possible to hear 20-year-old songs sounding totally new; everything the band plays is bursting with intensity." Santana also became involved in a number of charity concerts during the 1980s, and in 1988 he claimed his first Grammy Award—for best rock instrumental performance on the charity compilation album *Blues for Salvador.*

In 1989 Santana moved to Polydor Records because the company offered him an opportunity to start his own record label, Guts and Grace. His label's first release was an album called *Live Forever,* which featured songs from the last recorded concerts of the late musicians Jimi Hendrix, Marvin Gaye, Bob Marley, John Coltrane, and Stevie Ray Vaughn. "We wanted to create the atmosphere that they were all on the same stage doing it, at the same concert, and honor their music and spirit," he explained. By the early 1990s Santana's ongoing spiritual quest led him to become a born-again Christian, although he also incorporated teachings from other belief systems into his life philosophy.

Making a Comeback

During the 1990s Santana's early work continued to receive air play on classic rock radio stations, and his passionate live performances continued to thrill audiences. Music critics viewed him as a guitar virtuoso with a unique sound, and he was widely admired by fellow musicians and studied by young guitarists. In 1998 Santana and his original band were inducted into the Rock and Roll Hall of Fame. The statement announcing their selection read: "After nearly 30 years of musical growth and development, two things have remained constant: the fearless lead guitar of Carlos Santana and the fiery sound which is so identifiable and evocative—a fusion of blues, rock, Afro pan-Latino jungle rhythms, full-throttle vocals, and an always-danceable groove."

Despite such recognition, Santana felt that he had failed to connect with a new generation of fans. He realized that his work from the early 1970s formed the basis of his popularity, and he knew that he had not scored a radio hit since "Winning," from the 1981 album *Zebop!* Not content to settle for "legend" status as he entered his 50s, Santana began considering how to make a comeback. He claimed that an angel appeared to him at this time and told him to reach out to young listeners with positive music.

> "*Every musician who participated [in making* **Supernatural**] *was on the same wavelength and artistic energy as I was.* **Supernatural** *is a beautiful example of synchronicity. . . . Making it was a truly glorious experience.*"

In 1999 Santana signed a contract with Arista Records and began working on a new album—the 36th of his impressive career. He worked closely with producer Clive Davis, a longtime mentor who had signed him to his first record deal in 1969. Davis encouraged Santana to write some songs himself and collaborate with popular younger artists on others in order to attract new fans. Santana wanted all the songs to offer a hopeful message that would appeal to a large audience. "If you have the right song, you can reach out to junior highs, high schools, and universities, as well as grandparents and little kids," he noted. "The song's the key, and like a house, if it's built correctly, it will not only hold a family but a generation."

Santana had no trouble finding young artists who were eager to collaborate with him on the new album, which he called *Supernatural.* As it turned out, each of the artists he approached had admired the guitar legend's work for years. Hip-hop star Lauryn Hill, who sang "Do You Like the Way," called Santana "one of the great influences of my life." Wyclef Jean was so excited to participate that he agreed to provide a song, even though he had not yet written one. "I knew I was such a fanatic of the guy that all I had to do was see him and I'd know what to write," he recalled. "We got to the studio and the song ['Maria Maria'] just came to me." The album also

Supernatural.

saw Santana collaborate with Dave Matthews, Eagle-Eye Cherry, Everlast, Rob Thomas of Matchbox 20, and fellow guitar legend Eric Clapton. "Every musician who participated was on the same wavelength and artistic energy as I was," Santana noted. "*Supernatural* is a beautiful example of synchronicity. . . . Making it was a truly glorious experience."

Upon its release in the summer of 1999, *Supernatural* became a tremendous success. It sold an amazing 15 million copies in the United States and more than 25 million worldwide, making it one of the best-selling albums of all time. Its first single "Smooth," featuring Rob Thomas on vocals, spent 12 consecutive weeks in the No. 1 position on the *Billboard* charts to become the longest-running top single of the year. In a review for *Time* magazine, David E. Thigpen said that *Supernatural* drew "an uncommonly diverse coalition of fans: grizzled 1960s hippies; university kids who prefer

Dave Matthews but know a good jam when they hear one; Latin rockers lured by fiery guitar and tropical-tinged rhythms; and, as Santana himself describes them, 'kids who aren't as old as my Metallica T-shirt.'"

Supernatural went on to win eight Grammy Awards in 2000, tying Michael Jackson's 1983 record for the most awards won by an artist in a single year, for his mega-hit *Thriller*. The honors for *Supernatural* included album of the year, rock album of the year, and record of the year for "Smooth." In accepting one of the awards, Santana paid tribute to his humble origins. "This is for all the people who don't have running water or electricity," he stated. "If I could do it, you could do it." *Supernatural* also earned three Latin Grammy Awards and an American Music Award for best album.

> **"**
>
> *Following the release of* **Supernatural,** *Santana spoke publicly for the first time about the sexual abuse he endured as a teenager living alone in Tijuana. "Part of the reason* **Supernatural** *is such a fantastic phenomenon is because I chose to face my demons, fear, and pain. I opened the window and stood naked and said this thing happened to me and I'm not ashamed. I opened up that door to say, let's educate our children so this doesn't happen to anyone else."*
>
> **"**

Following the release of *Supernatural,* Santana spoke publicly for the first time about the sexual abuse he endured as a teenager living alone in Tijuana. "Part of the reason *Supernatural* is such a fantastic phenomenon is because I chose to face my demons, fear, and pain," he revealed. "I opened the window and stood naked and said this thing happened to me and I'm not ashamed. I opened up that door to say, let's educate our children so this doesn't happen to anyone else."

Santana's success has continued since the release of *Supernatural.* In 2002 he joined forces with a new group of artists—including Musiq, Seal, Michelle Branch, and Placido Domingo—on a similarly collaborative album called *Shaman.* His song with Branch, "The Game of Love," received a Grammy Award for best pop collaboration of the year. Santana repeated this formula for success with his 2005 album, *All That I Am,* featuring Los Lonely Boys, Mary J. Blige, and Big Boi. On his web site, Santana described his most recent album as "an extension and continuation of a vision co-created by Mr. Clive Davis and myself. We equate what we do with the dimen-

Santana performing at a benefit concert for victims of war.

sions of a three-ring circus . . . where children, teenagers, parents, and grandparents can share unity and harmony in the family of life. We create songs and magic pairing to bring joy and happiness to the listener." Also in 2005, Santana's song "Al Otro Lado Del Rio," which appeared on the soundtrack of the critically acclaimed film *The Motorcycle Diaries*, received an Academy Award for best original song.

Connecting with People through Music

By blending blues and rock music with Latin rhythms and adding his own flaming guitar, Carlos Santana created a passionate sound that helped him earn a devoted following and sell over 80 million albums to date. From the beginning, however, Santana has insisted that music is about self-expression and connecting with others rather than commercial success. He also believes that music has the potential to transform people's lives. "My intention has always been to make people laugh and cry and dance at the same time. When people reach that state, it's not just me playing. A whole other spirit takes over," he noted. "Our music continues to be tremendously appealing to all kinds of people — young, old, black, white, hip, square — and all cultures. I don't deliberately try to make it appealing to lots of different audiences. I just try to get to that next note, to get inside it so the listener can do the same."

> "*My intention has always been to make people laugh and cry and dance at the same time. When people reach that state, it's not just me playing. A whole other spirit takes over. Our music continues to be tremendously appealing to all kinds of people—young, old, black, white, hip, square— and all cultures. I don't deliberately try to make it appealing to lots of different audiences. I just try to get to that next note, to get inside it so the listener can do the same.*"

Known for his fiery guitar solos, Santana claims that the secret to making great music comes from investing heart and soul into a search for the perfect note. "A lot of times you may hit some really ugly notes, but that's okay in the pursuit of that perfect thing. That's the whole romance of losing and finding yourself when you take a solo. You must lose yourself to find yourself. If you approach everything from an analytical point of view, the mind takes over. By the time you do your solo, it might sound great, but it's not going to penetrate," he explained. "When I hit that note — if I hit it correctly — I'm just as important as Jimi Hendrix, Eric Clapton, or anybody. Because when I hit that note, I hit the umbilical cord of anybody who is listening."

MARRIAGE AND FAMILY

Santana married Deborah Sara King, the founder of a health food shop in San Francisco and daughter of blues guitarist Saunders King, in April 1973. They have three children: Salvador, Stella, and Angelica. Santana and his family live in a mansion in San Rafael, California, overlooking San Francisco Bay. "I'm just grateful that I can balance my music life and my family life," he stated. "My family is prime time, and everything else is secondary — including music."

HOBBIES AND OTHER INTERESTS

Throughout his career, Santana has contributed to charitable causes and participated in benefit concerts. "Playing music is easy, like drinking water. But changing the conditions of life is a little more challenging, and infinitely more rewarding," he stated. "The '60s taught me that if you aren't part of the solution, you're part of the problem. It's an old cliche, but I'd rather contribute to the solution." So in 1998 he and his wife formed the Milagro Foundation to support charities that improve the health care and educational opportunities available to underprivileged children around the world. In 2004 the foundation distributed more than $250,000 from the sale of concert tickets and albums to children's charities. "We feel very passionate — my wife and I — that we can make a difference," Santana said.

SELECTED ALBUMS

With Santana Band

Santana, 1969 (reissued 1998)
Abraxas, 1970 (reissued 1998)
Santana III, 1971 (reissued 1998)
Caravanserai, 1972
Welcome, 1973
Greatest Hits, 1974
Borboletta, 1974
Amigos, 1976
Festival, 1976
Moonflower, 1977
Marathon, 1979
Zebop! 1981
Viva Santana! 1988
Milagro, 1992
Dance of the Rainbow Serpent, 1995

Live at the Fillmore 1968, 1997
Best of Santana, 1998; Vol. 2, 2000
Supernatural, 1999
Shaman, 2002
All That I Am, 2005

Solo

Live Carlos Santana, 1972 (with Buddy Miles)
Love Devotion Surrender, 1973 (with John McLaughlin)
Illuminations, 1974 (with Alice Coltrane)
Havana Moon, 1983
Blues for Salvador, 1987
Spirits Dancing in the Flesh, 1990

HONORS AND AWARDS

Grammy Awards: 1988, best rock instrumental performance for *Blues for Salvador;* 2000 (eight awards), album of the year and rock album of the year for *Supernatural;* record of the year and best pop collaboration with vocals for "Smooth"; best rock performance by a duo or group for "Put Your Lights On"; best pop performance by a duo or group for "Maria Maria"; best rock instrumental performance for "The Calling"; and best pop instrumental performance for "El Farol"; 2002, best pop collaboration for "The Game of Love"

Chicano Lifetime Achievement Award: 1997

Golden Eagle Legend in Music Award (*Nosotros*): 1997

Rock and Roll Hall of Fame: 1998

Alma Award (National Council of La Raza): 1999

Medallion of Excellence for Community Service (Hispanic Congressional Caucus): 1999

Man of the Year (VH-1): 2000

Latin Music Awards: 2000 (three awards), album of the year for *Supernatural,* record of the year for "Corazon Espinado," and best pop instrumental performance for "El Farol"

American Music Award: 2000, album of the year for *Supernatural*

Blockbuster Entertainment Award for Favorite Rock Artist or Group: 2000

Person of the Year (Latin Academy of Recording Arts and Sciences): 2004

Hispanic of the Year (*Hispanic* magazine): 2004

Academy Award for Best Original Song: 2005, for "Al Otro Lado Del Rio," from the soundtrack to *The Motorcycle Diaries*

FURTHER READING

Books

Contemporary Hispanic Biography, Vol. 1, 2002
Contemporary Musicians, Vol. 43, 2003
Dictionary of Hispanic Biography, 1996
Grove Dictionary of Music and Musicians, 2001
Leng, Simon. *Soul Sacrifice: The Santana Story,* 2000
Remstein, Henna. *Latinos in the Limelight: Carlos Santana,* 2002 (juvenile)
Shapiro, Marc. *Carlos Santana: Back on Top,* 2000
Who's Who in America, 2005

Periodicals

Billboard, Oct. 5, 2002, p.1; Aug. 14, 2004, p.21
Current Biography Yearbook, 1998
Guitar Player, Jan. 1993, p.58; Aug. 1999, p.74; July 2003, p.25
Hispanic, Mar. 31, 1996, p.19; May 31, 2000, p.82; Dec. 2004, p.38
Los Angeles Times, Aug. 9, 1998, Calendar, p.3; Feb. 24, 2000, p.S1
Newsweek, Feb. 14, 2000, p.66
People, Feb. 28, 2000, p.97
Time, Oct. 25, 1999, p.120
Whole Earth, Summer 2000, p.72

Online Databases

Biography Resource Center Online, 2005, articles from *Contemporary Hispanic
    Biography,* 2004; *Contemporary Musicians,* 2003; *Dictionary of Hispanic
    Biography,* 1996
WilsonWeb, 2005, articles from *Current Biography,* 1998; *Grove Dictionary of
    Music and Musicians,* 2001

ADDRESS

Carlos Santana
Creative Artists Agency
9830 Wilshire Blvd.
Beverly Hills, CA 90212

WORLD WIDE WEB SITE

http://www.santana.com

Curt Schilling 1966-

American Professional Baseball Pitcher with the
Boston Red Sox
Overcame Injury to Help His Team Win the 2004
World Series

BIRTH

Curtis Montague Schilling was born in Anchorage, Alaska, on
November 14, 1966. He was one of three children born to Mary
Jo Schilling and Cliff Schilling, a career soldier in the U.S. Army.

YOUTH

Curt inherited an early love of baseball from his father, who placed a ball and glove in his infant son's crib. A native of Pennsylvania, Cliff Schilling was a huge fan of the city of Pittsburgh's professional sports teams, especially the Pirates (baseball) and the Steelers (football). Curt shared this passion from as far back as he can remember. "A lot of the best memories in my life revolve around my father and the Pirates or my father and the Steelers," he recalled. "Because I held my father in such high regard that anybody he talked that way about had to be superhuman to me."

Curt enjoyed playing baseball from an early age. In fact, an early family video shows him swinging a plastic bat when he was just two years old. Almost from the beginning, Curt could throw a baseball much harder than other kids his age. On many youth teams, the player with the strongest arm ends up playing third base, because the third baseman must make long throws across the diamond to first base. Curt started out at third base when he began playing organized baseball, but he always longed to become a pitcher like his favorite players, Nolan Ryan and J. R. Richard. "I always liked power pitchers when I was young, anybody with power," he remembered.

Curt started out at third base when he began playing organized baseball, but he always longed to become a pitcher like his favorite players, Nolan Ryan and J. R. Richard. "I always liked power pitchers when I was young, anybody with power," he remembered.

EDUCATION

Shadow Mountain High School

Growing up in a military family meant that Curt moved often and attended school in many different places as a child. After spending two years in Anchorage, the Schillings lived in Missouri, Kentucky, and Illinois before settling in Phoenix, Arizona. Curt loved living in sunny Phoenix, where he could play baseball every day. He attended Shadow Mountain High School, home to one of the best baseball programs in the state of Arizona. He played on the junior varsity team for his first three years of high school, still stuck at third base and close to giving up his dream of becoming a pitcher.

After his junior year, Schilling attended a major-league tryout camp put on by the Cincinnati Reds. The Reds' scouts narrowed the field of prospects by making all the players run a timed 40-yard dash. Schilling was not very fast, so he knew that he could not pass the speed trial. But the scouts did not require the pitching prospects to perform the speed trial, so he decided to try out as a pitcher. His very first pitch hit the catcher's mitt with such a loud "pop" that it turned heads all around the practice area, and every subsequent pitch made the same sound. When his tryout ended, the scouts informed him that his pitches had exceeded 90 miles per hour on their radar guns — a tremendous speed for a high-school player. The team was ready to discuss a formal tryout until they learned that Schilling had not yet graduated from high school.

During his senior year, Schilling pitched for the Shadow Mountain varsity team. Although he would have been the best pitcher on most high school teams, he was one of four equally talented pitchers for Shadow Mountain. This situation limited his opportunities to showcase his talents, but he decided that his own playing time was less important than his team's overall success. "I learned a valuable lesson," Schilling recalled. "I learned that no matter what you think is fair in life, sometimes it's not what somebody else sees. Whether it was fair or not that I didn't play varsity baseball until my senior year was beside the point."

Yavapai Junior College

After graduating from high school in 1985, Schilling decided to attend Yavapai Junior College, which boasted one of the best junior college teams in the country. Many former players had gone on to play at four-year colleges or had been drafted by the pros. But before he took the mound at Yavapai for the first time, Schilling learned that he had been selected by the Boston Red Sox in the January 1986 draft (at that time there were two baseball drafts each year, in January and in June; the January draft is no longer held). The Sox chose Schilling in the second round, shortly before his first season at Yavapai.

Although he was thrilled to be drafted, Schilling knew he had a lot to learn and decided to remain with his junior college team. It proved to be a good decision. Over the course of that season, Yavapai Coach David Dangler taught Schilling to throw his pitches at different speeds and angles, to use the same windup motion on each pitch, and to slow down and stay in control. These lessons helped Schilling post a 10-2 record in the regular season and lead his team to the top position in the national junior college (juco) rankings. Yavapai qualified for the Juco World Series, where the team finished third. "It was one of the greatest, most fun years of my life," he related. At the conclusion of his successful freshman season, Schilling decided to make the leap to professional baseball. Since Boston retained his rights for a year, he signed a contract with the Red Sox on May 30, 1986. He left college without earning a degree.

CAREER HIGHLIGHTS

Moving Up through the Minor Leagues

After being drafted by the Red Sox, Schilling was assigned to play in the minor leagues. Many baseball players start their careers in the minor leagues, also called the farm system. The teams in the minor leagues are affiliated with those in the major leagues. There are a variety of minor leagues, which are ranked according to the level of competition. The top or best league is Class AAA (called Triple A), next is Class AA, then Class A, then below that are the rookie leagues. Players hope to move up through the system to a Class AAA team and then to the major leagues.

Schilling was assigned to play first for Elmira in the Single-A New York—Pennsylvania League in 1986 and then earned a promotion to a higher Single-A team in Greensboro, North Carolina, in 1987. Off the field, however, he faced a more difficult adjustment. He had never lived on his own before, beyond the reach of his father's strict rules, and he suddenly found himself earning more money than he had ever seen. "My first month as a pro I made $6,000," Schilling recalled. "I took that check to the bank and got 300 $20 bills, threw them on the bed in my hotel room, and just lay there, watching TV." With a lack of supervision and an infusion of cash, he soon developed a reputation as a party-loving free spirit. He described his life in the minor leagues as being "like living in a frat house with no classes and getting paid for it. In all these little towns, where the ballpark is the center of things, you're a bigwig. That's a lot of power for a 19- or 20-year-old, and I played it for all it was worth."

> "My first month as a pro I made $6,000. I took that check to the bank and got 300 $20 bills, threw them on the bed in my hotel room, and just lay there, watching TV."

Following the 1987 season, Schilling's father was diagnosed with cancer and given only a few months to live. Curt was devastated by the news, since his father had always been his biggest supporter. In January 1988,

Cliff Schilling came to visit his son. The night before he was scheduled to return home, the two men talked into the wee hours of the morning. "We stayed up late that night just talking about baseball, life, everything," Curt recalled. "He said things that a father usually thinks, but doesn't say. I remember him saying how he knew I was going to make it to the big leagues."

The next morning, Cliff suddenly experienced severe chest pain, collapsed, and died in his son's arms. Curt later learned that he had experienced a burst aortic aneurysm (a weak spot in an artery to the heart). "Now I didn't have that calming voice to tell me everything was all right when I thought it wasn't," he said. Since his father's death, Schilling has come up with a unique way to honor his memory. At every game he starts, he leaves a ticket for his father at the gate as a symbolic gesture. Schilling says that he gets a feeling of inner peace by knowing that there is an empty seat in the stands reserved for his father.

> *Schilling described his life in the minor leagues as being "like living in a frat house with no classes and getting paid for it. In all these little towns, where the ballpark is the center of things, you're a bigwig. That's a lot of power for a 19- or 20-year-old, and I played it for all it was worth."*

As the 1988 season began, Schilling was promoted to the Red Sox's Double-A team in New Britain, Connecticut. He continued to pitch well, but his off-the-field behavior deteriorated even further. Concerned about his level of commitment, Red Sox management decided to trade him to the Baltimore Orioles' Double-A team in Charlotte. Unlike Boston, which had viewed him as a longshot to make the big leagues, Baltimore considered him one of its top prospects. Schilling received more attention and assistance than he ever had before, and it paid off. On September 1, when major-league teams were allowed to expand their rosters for the playoffs, the Orioles called him up to the big-league squad.

Major League Baseball — The Baltimore Orioles

When Schilling received that long-awaited call from the Orioles, he thought he was ready to play major league baseball. But he was still too interested in partying. "I was such a screw-up when I got to the big leagues," he admitted years later. "I was a total idiot. I ran the nightlife, I drank, I just acted crazy. I did all the stupid things you'd expect from a 21-year-old kid with money."

Schilling made his first major league start on September 7 against his original team, the Boston Red Sox. He pitched well, allowing three runs in seven innings to help the Orioles win by a score of 4-3. But he faltered in his other starts, finishing his first stint in the big leagues with no wins and an ERA above 10.00. He spent the next few years alternating between time in the big leagues and time in the minors, playing for the Orioles and their Triple-A team in Rochester, New York. At one point, after a series of poor performances, Manager Frank Robinson took the young pitcher aside and criticized his bad attitude, shoddy work ethic, and inattention to conditioning.

Schilling waits for the sign while pitching for the Houston Astros, 1991.

"He wasn't a bad kid," Robinson noted. "He just wanted to be noticed." The manager's talk had an influence on Schilling, and his behavior improved for the rest of the season.

In 1991 the Orioles traded Schilling to the Houston Astros. The Astros tried unsuccessfully to make the hard-throwing right-hander into a closer, a pitcher who comes in at the end of games, usually to protect a narrow lead. But Schilling had trouble with his control, walked a lot of hitters, and was demoted to the Astros' Triple-A team in Tucson, Arizona. Soon Houston lost patience with the young pitcher and traded him to the Philadelphia Phillies at the start of the 1992 season.

Reaching a Turning Point

Before he joined his new team, however, Schilling experienced a major turning point in his career. While working out at the Houston Astrodome during the off-season, he ran into Roger Clemens, a star pitcher for the Boston Red Sox who made his home in Texas. Schilling had met Clemens briefly when both players were with Boston, and he admired the Red Sox ace a great deal. Clemens was only four years older, but he had already won three Cy Young Awards as the American League's best pitcher. Schilling dreamed of following in Clemens's footsteps, so he was thrilled when a clubhouse attendant told him that Clemens wanted to talk to him.

But Schilling's excitement quickly turned to embarrassment. Instead of sitting and trading pitching tips with the superstar, Schilling was forced to listen quietly while an angry Clemens berated him for over an hour. Widely known as the hardest-working pitcher in baseball, Clemens had watched in disbelief as Schilling loafed his way through his off-season workout program. He criticized the struggling young player for wasting his enormous talent and disrespecting the game of baseball. Schilling felt humiliated, but he knew that everything Clemens said was true. He vowed to change that very day. Since that time, Schilling has credited "The Talk" with turning his career around. "I can't repeat a lot of what [Clemens] said," he noted. "He just railed at me. He said I was wasting my career and I was cheating the game. . . . It was one of the three or four most pivotal moments of my career. It was one of those conversations your father has with you when you're going down the wrong path and it saves your life."

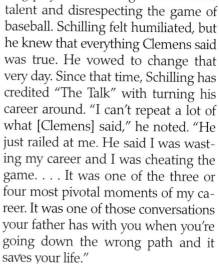

> "I can't repeat a lot of what [Clemens] said. He just railed at me. He said I was wasting my career and I was cheating the game. . . . It was one of the three or four most pivotal moments of my career. It was one of those conversations your father has with you when you're going down the wrong path and it saves your life."

The Philadelphia Phillies

When Schilling reported to the Phillies a few months later, he was a changed man. He came to training camp in the best shape of his career, and his improved strength and stamina paid off. Working his way into the starting lineup, he posted a career-high 14 victories (against 11 losses), with 10 complete games and an ERA of just 2.35.

In 1993 Schilling became one of the best pitchers in the National League. He finished the season with a 16-7 record and 186 strikeouts in 235.1 innings. The Phillies won the division and advanced to the National League Championship Series (NLCS), where they faced the heavily favored Atlanta Braves. Schilling had an outstanding series. As the starter in Game 1, he set a record by striking out the first five Braves he faced. He ended up

Schilling pitching for the Philadelphia Phillies, 1992.

striking out 10 and giving up only two runs in eight innings, to help the Phillies win the game by a score of 4-3 in 10 innings. Schilling achieved a similar result in Game 5 and was named NLCS Most Valuable Player for his role in helping the Phillies win the pennant.

Advancing to the World Series for the first time since 1983, the Phillies faced the Toronto Blue Jays. The two teams played an exciting World Series that featured a memorable finish. Toronto won three of the first four games in the best-of-seven series and seemed to be on its way to an easy title. Schilling took the loss in Game 1, which Toronto won 8-5. By the time he took the mound again in Game 5, he was asked to keep the Phillies alive in the series. He started out strong, regularly throwing fastballs clocked in the mid-90s on the radar gun. By the seventh inning he began to tire, and the speed of his pitches dropped into the mid-80s. But the Phillies had used so many pitchers the night before — in a heartbreaking 15-14 extra-inning loss — that there was no one available to relieve him. "I looked out in the bullpen and there was nobody there," he recalled. "I knew it was my game, and in many ways, that gave me the adrenaline to keep going." Schilling held on to finish a brilliant complete-game shutout and keep his team alive. His gutsy performance made him a folk hero in Philadelphia.

Unfortunately, the Phillies' reprieve lasted only one game. They lost the series on a home run in the bottom of the ninth inning in Game 6.

During the next two seasons, injuries limited his performance. In fact, Schilling only won a total of nine games in 1994 and 1995. Following the 1995 season he had surgery to repair tendon and rotator cuff damage in his shoulder. During this time, he rededicated himself to being the best pitcher he could be. He built a weight room in his house, improved his workout regimen, and began keeping a video record of every hitter he faced in order to aid his mental preparation. "When [the injuries] happened, it made me stop and think about how I want to be remembered when I'm done," he explained. "I'd like to be thought of as one of the best pitchers of my era."

Schilling's dedication paid off when he returned to the starting rotation in May 1996. Although his record was only 9-10, he struck out 182 batters in just 183.1 innings and led the league with eight complete games. By the end of the season, he was widely viewed as one of the toughest pitchers in baseball. Since his contract with Philadelphia was set to expire, a number of teams attempted to sign him as a free agent. Schilling was happy with the Phillies, however, and passed up higher salaries offered by other teams to remain in Philadelphia. "I make more money than I'll ever need," he admitted after signing a new contract.

Schilling had an outstanding year in 1997. He posted a record of 17-11 with a 2.97 ERA, made the All-Star team for the first time in his career, and broke J. R. Richard's record for most strikeouts by a right-handed pitcher in one season by fanning 319 batters. Schilling's strong performances continued in 1998 and 1999. He won 15 games and made the All-Star team in each of these seasons. His record in 1999 was even more impressive because he missed the last two months of the season after again undergoing arm surgery.

The Arizona Diamondbacks

In 2000, the Phillies decided to trade several veteran players for talented young prospects. Schilling was the Phillies' most valuable asset, and several teams expressed an interest in acquiring him. He was sent to the Arizona Diamondbacks, a talented team that was poised to make a run at the World Series. Combined with perennial All-Star Randy Johnson, Schilling gave Arizona one of the toughest starting pitching rotations in all of baseball. While Schilling had always enjoyed playing for the Phillies, he was excited at the prospect of making a playoff run with the Diamondbacks.

At first the trade appeared to be a mistake. Bothered by arm trouble, Schilling was unable to pitch his best in 2000. The Diamondbacks fell just short of making the postseason, and Schilling took much of the blame. "Ultimately I ended up being one of the reasons we didn't make the play-offs," he acknowledged. "I couldn't get it done." In 2001, however, he turned in a spectacular season. He posted a career-best 22-6 record and a 2.98 ERA, finishing second to Johnson in voting for the Cy Young Award. The two star pitchers combined for 665 strikeouts—the most strikeouts by teammates in a single season in baseball history. Johnson led the league with 372, while Schilling finished second with 293.

To people who knew baseball, it was obvious that each pitcher fed off the other's success. "Randy and Curt raised the bar for each other all year," said Arizona outfielder Luis Gonzalez. "You could see that when one of them pitched a good game, it was as if he said to the other one, 'Here you go, big guy. Now let's see what you can do.'" Led by Schilling and Johnson, the Diamondbacks cruised into the playoffs. After defeating the St. Louis Cardinals and the Atlanta Braves in the first two rounds, Arizona clinched a spot in the World Series, where they faced the legendary New York Yankees—the most successful team in baseball history. But Schilling refused to be intimidated by the Yankees' storied past.

> "Randy and Curt raised the bar for each other all year," said Arizona outfielder Luis Gonzalez. "You could see that when one of them pitched a good game, it was as if he said to the other one, 'Here you go, big guy. Now let's see what you can do.'"

The 2001 World Series

The Diamondbacks-Yankees World Series turned out to be one of the most memorable in baseball history, with the outcome decided in the bottom of the ninth inning of Game 7. The Diamondbacks took an early lead in the series by winning the first two games at home. Schilling led the way in Game 1, striking out eight Yankees in seven innings to earn the win in Arizona's 9-1 rout. "I know all about the history of the Yankees," he told reporters after the game, "but I wasn't pitching against Babe Ruth and Mickey Mantle today." Game 2 saw Johnson earn a victory by throwing a three-hit, 11-strikeout masterpiece to beat New York 4-0. But the Yankees came back strong to win the next three games in New York. With their opponents leading the series 3-2, the Diamondbacks faced two must-win

Schilling (in jacket) in the midst of a jubilant celebration after the Diamondbacks defeated the Yankees 3-2 to win Game 7 of the 2001 World Series.

games at home to claim the world championship. In Game 6, Johnson held the Yankees to just two runs, while Arizona scored early and often to trounce the Yankees by a score of 15-2.

Schilling took the mound for Arizona in the deciding Game 7, while the Yankees countered with the ace of their staff, 300-game-winner Roger

Clemens, whose reprimand nearly a decade earlier had helped Schilling turn his career around. In a gutsy performance, Schilling struck out nine batters to take a razor-thin 1-0 lead into the seventh inning. The Yankees finally got to him in that inning, tying the game on a single by Tino Martinez. In the eighth inning, Schilling got the first batter out but then watched in disgust as Alfonso Soriano hit a solo home run to put the Yankees ahead 2-1. Recognizing that Schilling had grown tired, Arizona Manager Bob Brenley decided to replace him with a relief pitcher. Amazingly, Brenley called upon starter Randy Johnson, who had just earned his second win of the series the day before. But Brenley's instincts proved correct, and Johnson retired the Yankees in the eighth and ninth innings without allowing any more runs.

To win the game and the title, the Diamondbacks had to score two runs against the best relief pitcher in baseball, Mariano Rivera, who had yet to allow a run in the series. The Arizona batters came through in dramatic fashion, sending the winning run home with two outs in the bottom of the ninth. Schilling was thrilled with his team's exciting World Series victory. "Nothing could be more meaningful than to beat the Yankees in the World Series," he said afterward. "This was great for baseball. We beat the best team in baseball to win a World Series. You just cannot imagine the feeling looking around our clubhouse and knowing the hard work that went into this." In recognition of his outstanding performance in the World Series, Schilling was named co-Most Valuable Player along with Johnson.

In the two years following Arizona's World Series win, Schilling continued to be one of the anchors of the Diamondbacks' pitching staff. In 2002 he went 23-7 with 313 strikeouts and once again finished second to Johnson in Cy Young Award voting. Although the two pitching aces led Arizona back to the playoffs, the team was swept in the first round by the St. Louis Cardinals. In 2003, Schilling missed more than two months of the season due to injuries and only compiled an 8-9 record. The Diamondbacks missed the playoffs that year and entered a rebuilding phase.

The Boston Red Sox

At the end of the 2003 season, the Diamondbacks started trading older, more expensive players, including Schilling, who was traded to the Boston Red Sox. Schilling welcomed the idea of returning to the team that had drafted him. He knew that Boston fans had waited 87 years for a World Series title, and he hoped to contribute to the team's success. "I love that people are counting on me to be a huge part of winning a World Series," he said. "That's why I'm here. I love the expectations. I have always felt the bigger the game, the better I get. I live on adrenaline. I want to be part of a team that does something that has not been done in almost a century."

Despite the enormous pressure he faced, Schilling delivered exactly what was expected of him in 2004. He led the American League with 21 wins and helped Boston clinch a wildcard playoff spot. Led by Schilling's 9-3 victory in Game 1, the Red Sox swept the defending World Series champion Anaheim Angels in the first round of the playoffs. Boston then faced the powerful New York Yankees in the American League Championship Series (ALCS).

"I love that people are counting on me to be a huge part of winning a World Series," Schilling said after he joined the Boston Red Sox. "That's why I'm here. I love the expectations. I have always felt the bigger the game, the better I get. I live on adrenaline. I want to be part of a team that does something that has not been done in almost a century."

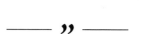

Defeating the Yankees

Schilling started Game 1 of the ALCS, but he was forced to leave the mound after three innings due to an ankle injury. The Yankees then cruised to a 10-7 win. Schilling's ankle had begun acting up during the Anaheim series, but he initially thought that it was a simple sprain. As it turned out, however, the injury was much more serious—he had suffered severe damage to a tendon that would require surgery to repair. The only question was whether Schilling could find a way to continue pitching through the playoffs on the injured ankle.

The Red Sox played poorly in Games 2 and 3 and fell behind the Yankees 3-0 in the best-of-seven series. In the century-long modern era of professional baseball, no team had ever come back from this sort of deficit to win a playoff series. At this point, it appeared that yet another season would end in bitter disappointment for Boston fans. To the amazement of many observers, however, the Red Sox rallied to win an exciting Game 4 by a score of 6-4 in the 12th inning. Boston claimed victory again the following day to close the gap to 3-2.

Suddenly, Schilling's ankle injury occupied the center of the baseball universe. Fans across the country wondered if he would be able to pitch in Game 6. No one outside of the Boston clubhouse knew how badly he was

Schilling pitching against the New York Yankees in Game 6 of the 2004 American League Championship Series.

hurt. To the delight of Red Sox fans, the team announced shortly before game time that Schilling would indeed start Game 6.

In one of the most courageous performances in sports history, Schilling pitched seven innings and allowed only four hits. Unable to use his normal throwing motion, he resorted to a variety of off-speed pitches and well-placed fastballs to keep the Yankee hitters at bay. He remained on the mound even after the stitches holding the dislocated tendon in his ankle tore out, turning his sock into a bloody mess. "When I saw blood dripping

Still on crutches after surgery, Schilling shows off the 2004 World Series trophy.

though the sock, and he's giving us seven innings in Yankee Stadium, that was storybook," Boston first baseman Kevin Millar said. By the time Schilling left the game, the Red Sox held a 4-2 lead that they maintained until the end. "It's at the top of the list among all the games I've pitched," he said afterward. The Red Sox went on to dominate Game 7, scoring six times in the first two innings on their way to a 10-3 victory.

The Boston Red Sox Win the World Series

Compared to the dramatic ALCS, the 2004 World Series seemed anticlimactic. Boston swept the St. Louis Cardinals in four straight games to win the team's first world title in 87 years. Schilling once again provided an emotional lift by pitching through pain to lead his team to victory. When he took the mound in Game 2, his dislocated tendon was again held together with stitches. As before, he bled through his sock (which is now on display in the Baseball Hall of Fame) but still managed to pitch six innings and shut down the opposing team. The Red Sox went on to win the game 6-2 and take a 2-0 lead in the series. Boston maintained its focus and won the next two games to claim the World Series title. "I'm so proud of being a part of the greatest Red Sox team in history," Schilling said afterward. He also felt relieved that his teammates had completed the sweep. "I was not going to pitch Game 6," he admitted. "I could not do it. I had lost too much strength in the ankle and was unable to get any push-off, even just walking around."

During the off-season, Schilling finally underwent surgery to repair his ankle. Although he started three games at the beginning of the 2005 season, his ineffective performances made it apparent that he had tried to come back too soon. He was forced to go on the disabled list, but returned to the starting rotation in July to help the Red Sox defend their world championship. At the start of the 2005 season, Schilling's career record stood at 185-125, with 2,765 strikeouts and an ERA of 3.35.

MARRIAGE AND FAMILY

Schilling met his wife, Shonda Brewer, while he was living in Baltimore and playing for the Orioles. She worked as an associate producer at a local television station. They married in 1992 and eventually had four children: Gehrig, Gabriella, Grant, and Garrison.

HOBBIES AND OTHER INTERESTS

Off the field, Schilling has many interests, including computer gaming and military history. He combined these interests to form a company, Multi-Man Publishing, that creates military strategy board games. Schilling also collects military artifacts, especially from World War II, and baseball memorabilia, including a uniform and other items once owned by one of his heroes, Lou Gehrig.

Schilling is also active in charity work, with a particular interest in helping people with ALS (amyotrophic lateral sclerosis). Better known as Lou Gehrig's disease, because the legendary Yankee slugger died from it, ALS is a degenerative illness that affects the muscles. In 1992 Schilling founded Curt's Pitch for ALS, through which he donates $1,000 for every victory and $100 for every strikeout to support ALS charities. He also encourages corporate sponsors and baseball fans to donate money. Curt's Pitch has raised millions for ALS research. Schilling has also worked with the Shade Foundation to raise funds to support research into melanoma, a form of skin cancer; his wife, Shonda, was diagnosed with the disease in 2001. "The memories you create on a ball field are pretty insignificant things compared to the changes you can make in the life of a person," he said of his commitment to charity work.

HONORS AND AWARDS

Most Valuable Player, National League Championship Series: 1993
Lou Gehrig Award: 1995
Major League All-Star Team: 1997, 1998, 1999, 2001, 2002, 2004
Branch Rickey Award: 2001
World Series Championship: 2001 (with Arizona Diamondbacks), 2004 (with Boston Red Sox)
World Series Co-Most Valuable Player: 2001 (with Randy Johnson)
Jim "Catfish" Hunter Humanitarian Award: 2001
Hutch Award: 2001
Roberto Clemente Award: 2001
National League Pitcher of the Year (*Sporting News*): 2001, 2002
Sportsman of the Year Award (*Sporting News*): 2001

Co-Sportsman of the Year (*Sports Illustrated*): 2001 (with Randy Johnson), 2004 (with Boston Red Sox)
Philanthropist of the Year (*Worth Magazine*): 2002

FURTHER READING

Books

Hagen, Paul. *Curt Schilling: Phillie Phire!* 1999
Stout, Glenn. *On the Mound with . . . Curt Schilling,* 2004
Who's Who in America, 2005

Periodicals

People, June 1, 1998, p.73; Nov. 5, 2001, p.73
Sporting News, Dec. 17, 2001, p.8
Sports Illustrated, Feb. 2, 1998, p.78; Mar. 30, 1998, p.99; Nov. 12, 2001, p.36; Dec. 17, 2001, p.112; Nov. 1, 2004, p.48; Nov. 15, 2004, p.58
Time, Nov. 8, 2004, p.38
USA Today, June 22, 2001, p.C1; Oct. 26, 2001, p.C6; Aug. 28, 2002, p.C1; Mar. 15, 2004, p.C3; Oct. 20, 2004, p.C4; Feb. 24, 2005, p.C8; Mar. 9, 2005, p.C8

Online Databases

Biography Resource Center Online, 2005

ADDRESS

Curt Schilling
Boston Red Sox
4 Yawkey Way
Fenway Park
Boston, MA 02215

WORLD WIDE WEB SITES

http://boston.redsox.mlb.com
http://www.shadefoundation.org

Maria Sharapova 1987-

Russian Professional Tennis Player
Winner of the 2004 Wimbledon Women's Singles Title

BIRTH

Maria Sharapova (pronounced shah-rah-POH-vuh) was born
on April 19, 1987, in Nyagan, an industrial town in the Siberian
region of the former Soviet Union (now Russia). She is the
only child of Yuri Sharapova, who worked in the Siberian oil
fields, and his wife, Yelena Sharapova.

YOUTH

Maria's parents are originally from the part of the former Soviet Union that is now Belarus. About a year before she was born, the worst nuclear disaster in history took place at the Chernobyl nuclear power plant, just 50 miles from their home. One of the main reactors exploded at Chernobyl, killing 31 people and exposing countless others to dangerous levels of radiation. The explosion released 100 times more radiation than the atom bombs dropped on Japan to end World War II. This radiation contaminated the air, water, and soil in the surrounding area, leading to the immediate evacuation of over 100,000 people and the eventual resettlement of 200,000 more. To this day, people of the region continue to suffer high rates of cancer and other health problems due to radiation exposure.

> *When Martina Navratilova first saw Sharapova play, she was immediately impressed by the girl's potential. "It was not just in the way she played tennis," Navratilova recalled. "It was there in the way she moved, the way she walked, and the way she would kick a ball or pick it up and throw it. You cannot teach that fluidity or that ease of movement."*

Shortly before Maria was born, her parents left Belarus in order to escape the continuing fallout from the Chernobyl accident. They moved to a one-bedroom apartment in Nyagan, in western Siberia. When Maria was two years old, her family moved once again. This time they settled in Sochi, a resort town on the Black Sea, where Yuri Sharapova enjoyed playing tennis. Russia was experiencing a tennis boom around this time. Many Russians took up the sport after watching tennis in the 1988 Olympic Games (the sport's first appearance in the Games since 1924). The increased interest in tennis encouraged many towns to build tennis courts, which gave a generation of Russian youngsters greater opportunities to play.

As it turned out, Yuri Sharapova's tennis partner was the father of top-ranked Russian player Yevgeny Kafelnikov. He encouraged Yuri to introduce Maria to the game and even presented her with her first tennis racquet. From the beginning of her tennis career, Maria had a major advantage over other young players: she was ambidextrous, meaning that she could make shots equally well with either hand. In fact, her left hand was so strong that she almost became a left-handed player. To this day, her strong left hand makes her backhand a powerful weapon.

Moving to the United States

When Maria was five years old, she attended a children's tennis clinic in Moscow, where she attracted the attention of Czechoslovakian tennis legend Martina Navratilova. The winner of 18 Grand Slam singles titles during her long professional career, Navratilova was immediately impressed by the girl's potential. "It was not just in the way she played tennis," Navratilova recalled. "It was there in the way she moved, the way she walked, and the way she would kick a ball or pick it up and throw it. You cannot teach that fluidity or that ease of movement."

Navratilova suggested that Yuri Sharapova take his daughter to the United States so that she could train under top tennis coaches. In 1994 Maria's father took this advice, moving with his seven-year-old daughter to Bradenton, Florida. When they arrived, neither one spoke a word of English, and they had very little money. Due to visa problems, Maria's mother was not able to join them for two years.

Still, Yuri managed to arrange a tryout for Maria at the famous Bollettieri Tennis Academy, which has trained such top pros as Andre Agassi and Venus and Serena Williams. She impressed the coaches there, and they accepted her as a student. Yuri worked at odd jobs to pay the tuition, and Maria's grandparents sent money from Russia to help out. By the age of nine, Maria had earned a full scholarship to the academy, as well as a contract with the International Management Group (IMG) sports agency. "I had never seen a young woman with so much desire, so much maturity and focus," recalled IMG agent Gavin Forbes.

EDUCATION

Although Sharapova has never attended a traditional school, she has always been a good student. When she lived in Russia, her mother taught her at home. Once she moved to Florida, she completed the early years of her schooling at the Bollettieri Tennis Academy, where she lived in a dormitory with much-older girls and attended classes between tennis practice sessions. After turning professional in 2002, she began taking high-school equivalency courses through an Internet school. She had not yet completed her diploma by 2005.

CAREER HIGHLIGHTS

Turning Professional

Sharapova worked hard during her years at the Bollettieri Academy, determined to someday join the Women's Tennis Association (WTA) professional tour. At the age of 11, she began working with Robert Lansdorp, a highly regarded tennis coach who had previously trained such star players as Pete Sampras, Tracy Austin, and Lindsay Davenport. The head of the tennis academy, Nick Bollettieri, predicted that Sharapova's toughness would take her a long way. "She is extremely strict, disciplined, and a perfectionist," the coach explained. "She plays tennis like she's preparing for an attack, a battle. That's Maria Sharapova. There is no monkey business. Every shot has a purpose. She runs for every single, solitary ball."

>
>
> *"She is extremely strict, disciplined, and a perfectionist," explained Nick Bollettieri, head of the tennis academy. "She plays tennis like she's preparing for an attack, a battle. That's Maria Sharapova. There is no monkey business. Every shot has a purpose. She runs for every single, solitary ball."*

Sharapova achieved her goal of becoming a professional tennis player in 2002, at the age of 14. She made her debut on the professional circuit as an unranked player, but she performed well enough in her first few junior tournaments to receive a wildcard invitation to a WTA senior event at Indian Wells. After defeating a player ranked number 302 in the world in the first round of that event, Sharapova joined the WTA rankings at number 532. The rookie went on to win three singles titles that year at tournaments in Gunma, Japan; Vancouver, Canada; and Peachtree City, Georgia. Sharapova quickly advanced through the world rankings, ending her first season at number 186.

Over the course of her breakthrough 2003 season, Sharapova improved her WTA ranking by 154 spots, ending the year at number 32 in the world. Her strong showing in qualifying tournaments enabled her to play in her first Grand Slam events that year. There are many tournaments on the professional circuit of the Women's Tennis Association (WTA), but there are four prestigious tournaments that make up the Grand Slam of tennis: the French Open (also called Roland Garros), the Australian Open, Wim-

Sharapova in her first match on the WTA Tour, at Indian Wells, California, against Monica Seles. She was just 14.

bledon (in England), and the U.S. Open. So it was a great honor for Sharapova, ranked number 88 in the world by June 2003, to receive a wild-card invitation from the tournament committee to play at Wimbledon. She responded with the best performance of her young career, beating players ranked 21 and 11 to advance to the fourth round of the prestigious tournament. Sharapova's appearance in the quarterfinals was the best-ever showing by a wild-card player in Wimbledon history.

Due to age restrictions for eligibility, Sharapova could only enter a limited number of events in 2003. Nevertheless, she managed to claim her first WTA Tour title in September at the Japan Open. In fact, she won both the singles and doubles championships (playing with first-time partner Tamarine Tanasugarn of Thailand) in that event. In the singles competition, Sharapova overcame a 5-2 deficit in the determining third set to become the youngest player to win a WTA Tour event that year. Sharapova claimed a second WTA Tour title in November at the Bell Challenge in Quebec, Canada.

In women's tennis, a player wins a match by defeating her opponent in 2 out of 3 sets, while men must win 3 of 5 sets. The first player to win 6 games usually wins the set, but if their margin of victory is less than 2 games, the set is decided by a tie-breaker. Shorthand notation is often used to show the score of a tennis match. For example, 6-2, 4-6, 7-6 means that the player in question won the first set by a score of 6 games to 2, lost the next set 4 games to 6, and came back to win the match in a third-set tie-breaker.

Winning at Wimbledon

Sharapova started off the 2004 season with a bang by advancing to the third round of the Australian Open. In the second Grand Slam event of the year, the French Open, she made it to the quarterfinals. Although few experts expected the young Russian to win a Grand Slam title so early in her career, her performances in these important tournaments attracted attention in the tennis world. Some analysts predicted that Sharapova would make an especially strong showing at Wimbledon. They noted that her skills — such as quickness, a flat volley, and a preference for slice rather than topspin serves — were well-suited to the slow and often frustrating grass surface. Sharapova raised expectations considerably by winning a grass-court tournament in Birmingham, England, just two weeks before Wimbledon.

Sharapova entered the 2004 Wimbledon tournament as the 13th seed. She quickly proved herself, dispatching each of her opponents in the first four rounds without ever losing a set. In the semifinals, Sharapova defeated 1999 Wimbledon champion Lindsay Davenport 2-6, 7-6, 6-1 to claim her first career victory over a player ranked in the top five. The young Russian thus advanced to her first Grand Slam final, where she faced three-time Wimbledon champion Serena Williams. One of the most dominant players on the WTA Tour, the 22-year-old Williams had won the prestigious tournament the two previous years.

The women's final took place on July 3. Sharapova won the coin toss before the start of the match and confidently elected to serve. Her strong serve turned out to be an important factor in the match: she averaged 97 miles per hour, which was 11 miles per hour faster than her opponent's average, and chalked up 14 aces (unreturnable serves). Bolstered by her serve, Sharapova won five straight games on her way to taking the first set by a score of 6-1. Williams rallied to take a 4-2 lead in the second set, but Sharapova recovered and won four straight games to end the match in two sets. She completed her 6-1, 6-4 upset victory in only 73 minutes.

After the match ended, Williams told reporters that she had strained a muscle in her abdomen during the first game. She claimed that the injury had forced her to play in intense pain and had limited her to 20 percent of her

ABOVE: Sharapova facing Serena Williams in the finals at Wimbledon, 2004.

LEFT: Sharapova celebrating with her father after defeating Williams to win at Wimbledon.

BELOW: Sharapova and Williams share a celebratory moment after the match.

usual ability for the remainder of the match. But Sharapova did not let her opponent's comments detract from her accomplishment. After serving for championship point, she ran to the grandstands and hugged her father, Yuri. She tried to reach her mother—who, for superstitious reasons, never attends her matches—on a cellular phone, but was unable to get through. "It's amazing," Sharapova said upon accepting her Wimbledon trophy. "I never, never in my life expected this to happen so fast. It's always been my dream to come here and win, but it was never in my mind that I would do it this year."

Sharapova's Wimbledon championship earned her several spots in the record books. She became the third-youngest winner in the tournament's 127-year history, the lowest-seeded winner in the "Open Era" (since the four Grand Slam events gained additional status), and the first Russian player ever to win at Wimbledon. She also became the fourth-youngest player ever to win any of the Grand Slam events, and only the second Russian woman ever to win a Grand Slam title.

> *Sharapova was determined not to let her rising celebrity status sway her focus from the game. "The first thing I tell my sponsors is how many days I have in the year to do what they want me to do," she stated.*

Becoming a Media Darling

After her stunning victory at Wimbledon, Sharapova suddenly found herself in high demand by both sports and entertainment media. In fact, she received over 300 photo and interview requests over the next few weeks. Some reporters referred to the media onslaught as "Maria Mania." "A lot of people want a piece of me," she acknowledged. "It's been crazy. I've got photographers running around me and driving behind our car all the time." Sharapova made a number of high-profile television appearances, giving interviews on CBS's "Early Show," NBC's "Today Show," "Live with Regis and Kelly," and "The Tonight Show with Jay Leno." She also played table tennis (Ping-Pong) on MTV's "TRL."

In the print media, Sharapova was the subject of feature stories in *Italian Vogue* and *Hello!* magazines, and she became the first tennis player in over two years to appear on the cover of *Sports Illustrated*. As a reflection of her overnight stardom, her name became the third-most-popular search term on Yahoo! (after Jennifer Lopez and Britney Spears) in the weeks following Wimbledon.

Sharapova's photogenic appeal won her many endorsement contracts, including one with Canon for its digital cameras.

Sharapova also started receiving countless offers of endorsement contracts and modeling work. Some observers claimed that Sharapova's photogenic appeal would give women's tennis a much-needed boost. "Women's tennis has been looking for a new hero, a fresh face, and she embodies everything marketers and mainstream corporations are looking for," said sports agent Keith Kreiter. "She is beautiful, young, very well-spoken, and her story is quite remarkable." Although insiders noted that Sharapova could earn as much as $10 million per year in endorsements if her success continued, she was determined not to let her rising celebrity status sway her focus from the game. "The first thing I tell my sponsors is how many days I have in the year to do what they want me to do," she stated.

Getting Back to Business

After winning the 2004 Wimbledon championship, Sharapova had high hopes for the last Grand Slam event of the year—the U.S. Open in Flushing Meadows, New York. But she struggled on the hard, fast surface. After barely beating a lower-ranked opponent in the first round, she was knocked out by Mary Pierce in the third round.

The WTA Tour Championships in November featured a rematch between the two Wimbledon finalists. Sharapova once again prevailed over Serena Williams, 4-6, 6-2, 6-4. Sharapova became the second-youngest player ever to win the tournament and claimed $1 million in prize money. By the end of the 2004 season she had reached number 4 in the WTA world rankings. Her success led to her being named the WTA Tour's most improved player and player of the year.

At the first Grand Slam event of the 2005 season, the Australian Open, Sharapova defeated Svetlana Kuznetsova in the quarterfinals, 4-6, 6-2, 6-2. Advancing to the semifinals for the second time in her last three Grand Slam appearances, she faced Serena Williams once again. This time, however, Williams prevailed. Still, Sharapova's performance earned her enough points to take over the number 3 spot in the world rankings. By April she had improved her WTA ranking to number 2.

Sharapova turned in another strong performance at the 2005 French Open. She reached the quarterfinals of the tournament for the second year in a row before losing to tenth-seeded Justine Henin-Hardenne, 6-4, 6-2. In June 2005 Sharapova made a highly anticipated return to Wimbledon to defend her title. The champion roared through the early rounds of the tournament without losing a set. In fact, an opponent broke her serve (won a game in which Sharapova was serving) only one time in 44 service games. Sharapova thus reached the semifinals, where she faced Venus Williams — the older sister of Serena Williams, her finals opponent from the previous year. Venus Williams broke Sharapova's serve four times and also seemed to break the young Russian's spirit in handing her a hard-fought 6-7, 1-6 defeat.

Staying Tough

As an attractive, lean, six-foot blonde, Sharapova is often compared to fellow Russian player Anna Kournikova. Unlike Kournikova, who never won a major tournament and depended on her good looks as the source of her popularity, Sharapova downplays her looks and wants to be known for her tennis. "I never considered myself a pinup," she explained. "I never will."

Sharapova has also been compared to another former tennis player, Monica Seles, who shared her tendency to grunt loudly when hitting the ball. When several players complained about her noisy habit, Sharapova worked to scale back her outbursts, but she maintains her aggressive, confident style of play. "Whether she's down or whether it gets close or the pressure's on, she keeps hitting harder, keeps going for her shots," said ESPN analyst Mary Joe Fernandez. "The concentration is there all the time. That's what's separating her from the rest of them."

Finally, Sharapova has been compared to American tennis great Jimmy Connors for her mental toughness and determination. This trait has helped her earn the nicknames "Russian Steel" and "The Iron Maiden." Her long-time coach, Robert Lansdorp, argues that Sharapova's determination will help her overcome the pressure of being on top. "She's a sharp girl who knows how to control what she wants," he stated. "Maria is going to do what Maria wants to do. She will succeed the way Maria wants to succeed. She's a lot more mature than people think she is."

Some experts claim that Sharapova is well-positioned to become the next dynasty in women's tennis. "I think she's the most refreshing player to come along in years," said commentator Bud Collins. "No excuses. No shyness. And she just loves what she's doing." Sharapova credits her competitive nature and self-confidence for her success. "I love playing tennis, but I also love competing," she noted. "If you're going to be scared when you walk on the court, you already have a losing mentality. I believe in myself all the time."

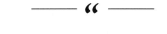

> *Sharapova credits her competitive nature and self-confidence for her success. "I love playing tennis, but I also love competing. If you're going to be scared when you walk on the court, you already have a losing mentality. I believe in myself all the time."*

HOME AND FAMILY

Sharapova is single and lives in Florida with her parents. Although she has resided in the United States for many years, she retains her Russian citizenship. Sharapova is very close to her parents, and she describes her mother as her best friend. "The move to the U.S. was an amazing sacrifice," she acknowledged. "Definitely I owe my parents a lot. They always wanted me to be happy, to go in the right direction in life. But there is no pressure from them. Who has an opportunity in life like I do right now at the age I am? Not too many people. At moments like these, I can return my family with favors."

HOBBIES AND OTHER INTERESTS

In her spare time, Sharapova enjoys fashion and designs her own tennis clothes. She also enjoys yoga, singing, dancing, watching movies, and collecting stamps.

HONORS AND AWARDS

Wimbledon, Women's Singles: 2004
WTA Tournament, Women's Singles: 2004
WTA Most Improved Player: 2005
WTA Player of the Year: 2005

FURTHER READING

Books

Who's Who in America, 2005

Periodicals

Detroit Free Press, July 1, 2005, p.D1
ESPN Magazine, June 20, 2005 (cover story)
Miami Herald, June 28, 2004
New York Times, July 4, 2004, p.1; July 5, 2004, p.3
People, Sep. 1, 2003, p.98
Sports Illustrated, July 12, 2004, p.46; July 26, 2004, p.58
Sports Illustrated for Kids, Sep. 2004, p.13
Tennis, May 2004, p.40
Time International, Sep. 1, 2003, p.52
USA Today, Jan. 13, 2004, p.C1; Aug. 30, 2004, p.C1; Nov. 16, 2004, p.C10;
   Jan. 25, 2005, p.C11

Online Databases

Biography Resource Center Online, 2005

ADDRESS

Maria Sharapova
WTA Tour
One Progress Plaza
Suite 1500
St. Petersburg, FL 33701

WORLD WIDE WEB SITE

http://www.wtatour.com/players

Ashlee Simpson 1984-
American Singer and Actress
Creator of the Hit Album *Autobiography* and Star of
MTV's "Ashlee Simpson Show"

BIRTH

Ashlee Nicole Simpson was born on October 3, 1984, in Waco,
Texas. Her father, Joe Simpson, was a Baptist minister who
specialized in counseling troubled youth. Her mother, Tina
Simpson, was an aerobics instructor. Ashlee has one sister, the
singer and reality-television star Jessica Simpson, who is four
years older.

YOUTH

Throughout her childhood, Ashlee often found herself in the shadow of her beautiful, talented, and well-behaved older sister. In order to gain attention, Ashlee sometimes acted up. As a little girl, for example, she walked barefoot into her father's church, made her way to the altar, and proceeded to pull up her dress in front of the entire congregation. In general, though, Ashlee considered her actions more "edgy" than bad. "I'm not the evil sister," she explained. "I'm the sister who's a little more out there." Ashlee is also quick to note that sibling rivalry did not ruin her childhood. "People always seem to think that I struggled because I was the younger sister," she noted. "Sure, I wanted attention occasionally, but we were such a close family, and Jessica and I were the best of friends."

———— " ————

"People always seem to think that I struggled because I was the younger sister. Sure, I wanted attention occasionally, but we were such a close family, and Jessica and I were the best of friends."

———— " ————

Both Ashlee and Jessica loved to sing in their youth. But while Jessica often sang in public — she joined the church choir at age five and quickly became a soloist — Ashlee usually restricted her performances to the privacy of her bedroom. "I would sing behind closed doors growing up," she remembered. "Jessica was so good and it made me shy about my own voice."

The two girls also favored different types of music. "Jessica and I are night and day," Ashlee acknowledged. "She grew up listening to Celine Dion and Mariah Carey. I grew up listening to Alanis Morissette and Green Day."

The first album Ashlee ever bought — at age 11 and without her mother's permission — was Morissette's alternative-rock *Jagged Little Pill*. She also has fond memories of attending the women's alternative music festival Lilith Fair when she was young. As she watched artists like Joan Osborne and Jewel perform, she knew that she wanted to grow up to be like them.

When Ashlee was young, though, she mostly wanted to become a dancer. She first began taking classical ballet lessons at age three, and at age 11 she became the youngest dancer ever accepted to the prestigious School of American Ballet in New York City. This was a tremendous opportunity, but it required her to move away from her family in Texas and live in a dormitory in New York for two years. She showed enough promise as a dancer that she was invited to study at the prestigious Kirov Ballet in Russia, but her father would not let her go so far away.

Supporting Her Sister

In the meantime, Ashlee's sister Jessica was vaulting to stardom. At the age of 12, Jessica was one of over 30,000 girls nationwide to audition for a spot on the musical-entertainment TV series "The New Mickey Mouse Club." Jessica's five-octave vocal range carried her to the finals, but she froze after hearing Christina Aguilera perform and was not selected to appear on the show. A few years later, however, Jessica was discovered by Tommy Mottola, chairman and CEO of Sony Music Entertainment, who signed her to a record deal.

While Ashlee was continuing her ballet training, her father decided to move the family to Los Angeles, California, in hopes of promoting Jessica's singing career. Ashlee did not mind leaving the School of American Ballet, and she instead turned her attention toward becoming an actress. Within two weeks of moving to Los Angeles, Ashlee had secured an agent and started auditioning for television commercials. Her first commercial was for the Kohl's department store.

In 1999, when Ashlee was 14, the entire Simpson family accompanied Jessica on her first concert tour. Jessica started out as the opening act for the band 98 Degrees, which featured her future husband, Nick Lachey. Grateful to her sister for accepting the move to California, Jessica asked Ashlee to be one of her backup dancers. Ashlee performed with her sister for the next three years.

After opening for several other prominent musical acts, Jessica finally got an opportunity to headline her own concert tour in 2002. The "Dream-chaser" tour was a spectacular success, cementing Jessica's status as one of the rising stars of pop music. By this time, though, Ashlee had begun exploring ways to step out of her sister's shadow. "There were times that it was hard being on tour," she admitted. "My sister was the celebrity pop star, and I just felt like I wanted to do my own thing a lot of the time. I was so sick of everyone telling me you have to look like this, dance like this." These feelings convinced Ashlee that it was time for her to stake out her own identity.

EDUCATION

Ashlee attended Prairie Creek Elementary School while she lived in Texas, then spent two years at the School of American Ballet in New York City. After the age of 14, she obtained much of her education on the road, doing homework between her sister's shows. She nevertheless excelled in her studies and earned her high school diploma by the time she was 16.

*Ashlee Simpson as Cecilia, David Gallagher as Simon Camden,
and Happy the dog in a scene from "7th Heaven."*

CAREER HIGHLIGHTS

Turning Her Focus to Singing

Although she loved the limelight of show business, Simpson was initially hesitant to follow her older sister into the music business. Instead, she focused on building an acting career. Some of her early roles included a guest appearance on the Emmy Award-winning television program "Malcolm in the Middle" in 2000, and a small role in the movie *The Hot Chick* in 2001. Simpson's big break came in 2002, when she received a recurring role on the televised family drama "7th Heaven." The show centered around a minister, Eric Camden, and his large family. Simpson played Cecilia Smith, a girlfriend of one of the Camden sons, Simon (played by David Gallagher). Originally signed to appear in just seven episodes, Simpson was featured on the series for two years, thanks to her popularity with the teen audience.

In an interesting twist of circumstances, Jessica then followed Ashlee into the television business. Jessica had married Nick Lachey in October 2002, when the "reality television" craze was just beginning. Joe Simpson encouraged his daughter to capitalize on the trend. He believed that musical artists could only increase their popularity by letting fans into their personal lives. "I believe reality TV has made America go, 'I want to know you before I buy your record,'" he explained. In the spring of 2003, the reality program "Newlyweds: Nick and Jessica" began airing on MTV. True to her father's predictions, the show became very popular and helped Jessica's musical career reach new heights.

That same year, Ashlee finally got up the nerve to pursue her own music career. "I think that if you love something so much you have to do it," she explained. "I love music so much, there was no choice." Her first recording was the song "Just Let Me Cry," which appeared on the soundtrack to the Disney movie *Freaky Friday*. Following the success of this record, Simpson decided to leave television and dedicate herself to music, which would allow her to better express her own views and emotions. But it took a lot of courage. "When you act, you're in a role," she noted. "If they [the viewers] don't like the character you play, it doesn't mean they don't like you. When you make an album of your own music, you're putting everything on the line."

Making Her First Album

Simpson signed a recording contract with Geffen Records in 2003 and began working on her first album. She drew upon her years of personal journal-keeping and her background as an actress to write all of the songs for the album herself. "My acting experience really helped me get into the characters of the songs and be in the moment with them," she explained. "I was able to go back to the events I'm singing about and bring them to life." One of the first songs she wrote, called "Shadow," was about growing up as the younger sister of a celebrity. The lyrics describe how Ashlee was able to escape from Jessica's shadow and follow her own dreams: "It used to be so hard being me / Living in the shadow / Of someone else's dream / But now that I am wide awake / My chains are finally free / Don't feel sorry for me."

It was clear from the beginning that Ashlee's album would bear little resemblance to the work of her sister. For one thing, Ashlee's voice and singing style were very different from Jessica's. In fact, Ashlee's voice was more similar to the raspy and raw delivery of popular singers from the 1980s, like Pat Benatar and Joan Jett. And unlike Jessica's straightforward pop sound, Ashlee's album covered several musical genres, including rock and punk. "I just wanted to go in and make a record and not worry about what genre it would be," she noted. "I went in to have a good time and I did. It's a rock record, with a cool edge to it. It's the first time people are getting to hear what I sound like." Ashlee collaborated with a number of

Simpson working on her album in a scene from her MTV reality series "The Ashlee Simpson Show."

other artists on the album, including Sugar Ray, Good Charlotte, and John Feldman from Goldfinger. Finally, to differentiate herself as much as possible from her blonde sister, Ashlee dyed her hair brunette when she launched her musical career, although she later dyed it blond.

In one respect, however, Ashlee did follow in Jessica's footsteps: she launched a reality TV show to help generate interest in her album. "The Ashlee Simpson Show" began airing on MTV in June 2003. It proved very popular, and within a few episodes it moved into the top five programs for 12- to 34-year-olds on cable television. The program followed Simpson through the personal trials and triumphs involved in making and launching her record album. "The show was a success because Ashlee came across as a real person and not as a glamorous star," said Brian Graden, president of entertainment for MTV Networks Music Group. "The music she made was truly expressive of the kinds of things she was going through at that time, and that kind of connection with viewers made it much more powerful." "At the end of the day, you see the successes and what it took to get there," Simpson added. "It's important to get yourself out there so that people know you as a person and not just the music."

A month before the launch of her debut album, Simpson released the single "Pieces of Me." Thanks in part to the success of "The Ashlee Simpson Show," the song received a great deal of radio airplay and raised expectations for the album. *Autobiography* was finally released on July 20, 2004. Despite receiving mixed reviews, the album sold a phenomenal 400,000 copies in its first week. It hit No. 1 on the pop charts on July 28 and stayed there for three weeks. It eventually went triple platinum, meaning that it sold over 3 million copies. *Autobiography* was one of the top 10 albums of 2004 in terms of sales, and it was also ranked among *Blender* magazine's "50 Greatest CDs of 2004." The album's success helped Simpson win Teen Choice Awards for Fresh Face of the Year and Song of the Summer.

Damaging Her Reputation

Following the tremendous success of *Autobiography,* Simpson's musical career seemed to be flying high. The album's popularity led to an invitation for Simpson and her band—Ray Brady and Braxton Olita on guitar, Zach Kennedy on bass, and Chris Fox on drums—to perform on the late-night comedy television program "Saturday Night Live." Unfortunately, this live TV appearance turned into a public relations nightmare for Simpson.

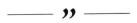

"The show was a success because Ashlee came across as a real person and not as a glamorous star," said Brian Graden, president of entertainment for MTV Networks Music Group. "The music she made was truly expressive of the kinds of things she was going through at that time, and that kind of connection with viewers made it much more powerful."

Simpson and her band were featured as musical guests on "Saturday Night Live" on October 23, 2004, performing twice. For their first appearance of the night, they performed "Pieces of Me." For their second appearance, the band started to play the introduction to the song "Autobiography." Then a pre-recorded backing track started to play Simpson's voice singing "Pieces of Me," which they had performed earlier. When the musical mismatch occurred, Simpson initially looked around as if confused. Then she danced a little jig on the stage, as if to make a joke out of the incident. Finally, though, she ran off the stage in embarrassment.

Simpson later claimed that she had suffered a bout of acid reflux, a condition in which stomach acid makes its way backward through the digestive

tract toward the throat. She said that the acid reflux had irritated her vocal chords and compromised her ability to sing. Rather than canceling the "Saturday Night Live" appearance, she decided to pretend to sing (or "lip synch") while her voice played on a backing track. While many singers choose to lip synch at times, the practice is generally frowned upon. After all, when fans pay for concert tickets, they expect to hear their favorite artists performing live. In addition, the use of backing tracks tends to make fans wonder if the voice they hear on an album really belongs to the artist, or if it was created in a music studio through special effects.

Simpson's decision to lip synch on "Saturday Night Live"—a program that built its reputation on live comedy sketches and musical performances—proved especially controversial. The incident received extensive coverage in the media and made her the target of both jokes and criticism.

But Simpson tried to take the negative attention in stride. "I don't regret that happening," she said of the incident. "I'm really glad that it did because it made me stronger. And when you have everybody trying to ask you questions about it and kind of tear you down about it, it helped me grow as an artist because I was finally like, 'I don't care. I'm young. I'm 20. And I'm learning. I'm a new artist. I'm just doing my thing.'" Simpson's father argued that her mistake paled in comparison with those made by other singing sensations. "She didn't expose a boob, she wasn't doing drugs, she isn't anorexic, and she didn't get married in Vegas," Joe Simpson declared.

Bouncing Back

Two days after her ill-fated "Saturday Night Live" appearance, Simpson rebounded to sing live at the Radio Music Awards. In December 2004 she was honored as the best new female artist at the Billboard Music Awards. She suffered another minor setback in January 2005, when she was invited to perform at halftime of the Orange Bowl college football game. Her rendition of "La La" did not go over well with the fans in the stadium, who booed loudly during her performance. Supporters pointed out, however, that Orange Bowl attendees don't fit the typical profile of most Ashlee Simpson fans.

Simpson also continued to dabble in acting. She appeared in an episode of "American Dreams" on NBC, for example, and also began shooting her first feature film. Originally titled *Wannabe*, the film was renamed *Undiscovered* following a legal battle over rights to the first name. Not coincidentally, "Undiscovered" is also the name of a song on Simpson's album. The independent film follows a group of aspiring actors and musicians trying to get their big breaks in Los Angeles. "The movie's all about music," Simpson explained. "I play an actress who's a tomboy type of girl, and music saves her from all the things that she deals with in her life."

—— **"** ——

"I don't regret that happening," Simpson said about the SNL lip-synching incident. "I'm really glad that it did because it made me stronger. And when you have everybody trying to ask you questions about it and kind of tear you down about it, it helped me grow as an artist because I was finally like, 'I don't care. I'm young. I'm 20. And I'm learning. I'm a new artist. I'm just doing my thing.'"

—— **"** ——

Ashlee with her family at the premier of her sister's movie The Dukes of Hazzard. *From left: Joe Simpson, Jessica Simpson, her husband Nick Lachey, Tina Simpson, and Ashlee.*

In the spring of 2005, both "The Ashlee Simpson Show" and "Newlyweds: Nick and Jessica" ceased production. But Ashlee has remained busy. She participated in the "Event to Prevent"—a concert held at Gotham Hall in New York to raise awareness of teen pregnancy—and appeared on the covers of *Allure, Teen People,* and *Cosmopolitan.* She remains very popular with her fans, the majority of whom are teenaged girls. Simpson's fans appreciate her warm, "everygirl" appeal, as well as her ability to act tough and "playfully naughty" at times. For her part, Simpson values her fans and tries to open herself up to them. "I think the most rewarding thing is playing shows now while fans are singing my songs at the top of their lungs with me," she said. "It's the coolest feeling. I always get chills. That's when everything is worth it. It's very cool."

HOME AND FAMILY

Simpson lives with her three best friends — Jen, Stephanie, and Lauren — in a house in Los Angeles that she bought from her parents.

Although some magazines have speculated about a difficult relationship between the Simpson sisters, Ashlee insists that she and Jessica are actually quite close. "I'm not jealous of her nor am I in competition with her," she said. "I'm proud of her, and I think that she's proud of me because she knows I've finally done what I wanted to do. And it took me a while to get there. My music is nothing like hers, so there's no competition there."

Both Ashlee and Jessica are managed by their father, Joe Simpson. Not unexpectedly, Joe has sometimes been accused of selfishly capitalizing on his daughters' talent. But he defends the active role he has played in promoting their careers. "I really try to wear three hats," he explained. "I try to wear my dad's hat — 'Is this going to hurt my child?' Then I put on a manager's hat and say 'Is this going to hurt my child's career?' and then I put on a television producer's hat and say, 'Is this good television?' We're always walking that line."

HOBBIES AND OTHER INTERESTS

In her spare time, Simpson enjoys going dancing or bowling with her roommates. She also likes to do crafts, like painting and knitting. Like her mother and sister, she loves to shop and has expressed an interest in one day starting her own clothing line.

SELECTED CREDITS

Recordings

Autobiography, 2004

TV Appearances

"Malcolm in the Middle," 2001
"7th Heaven," 2002-2003
"The Ashlee Simpson Show," 2003-2005
"American Dreams," 2004

Film Appearances

The Hot Chick, 2002
Undiscovered, 2005

HONORS AND AWARDS

Teen Choice Awards: 2004, for Fresh Face of the Year and Song of the Summer
Billboard Music Award: 2004, for Best New Female Artist
Breakout Star of the Year (*Entertainment Weekly*): 2004
Fun Fearless Female of the Year (*Cosmopolitan*): 2004

FURTHER READING

Books

Norwich, Grace. *Ashlee Simpson: Out of the Shadow and Into the Spotlight,* 2005 (juvenile)

Periodicals

Cosmopolitan, Feb. 2005, p.54
GQ, Jan. 2005, p.77
Pittsburgh Post-Gazette, Mar. 25, 2005, p.WE23
Seventeen, Nov. 2004, p.86
Teen People, Mar. 1, 2005, p.100
TV Week, Oct. 25, 2004, p.24
Vanity Fair, Jan. 2005, p.109

ADDRESS

Ashlee Simpson
Geffen Records
2220 Colorado Avenue
Santa Monica, CA 90404

WORLD WIDE WEB SITES

http://www.ashleesimpsonmusic.com
http://www.mtv.com/bands/az/simpson_ashlee/bio.jhtml

Photo and Illustration Credits

Cumulative Names Index

This cumulative index includes the names of all individuals profiled in *Biography Today* since the debut of the series in 1992.

For cumulative general, places of birth, and birthday indexes, please see biographytoday.com.

For cumulative general, places of birth, and birthday indexes, please see biographytoday.com.

Biography Today
General Series

*B*iography Today **General Series** includes a unique combination of current biographical profiles that teachers and librarians — and the readers themselves — tell us are most appealing. The **General Series** is available as a 3-issue subscription; hardcover annual cumulation; or subscription plus cumulation.

Within the **General Series**, your readers will find a variety of sketches about:

- Authors
- Musicians
- Political leaders
- Sports figures
- Movie actresses & actors
- Cartoonists
- Scientists
- Astronauts
- TV personalities
- and the movers & shakers in many other fields!

"*Biography Today* **will be useful in elementary and middle school libraries and in public library children's collections where there is a need for biographies of current personalities. High schools serving reluctant readers may also want to consider a subscription.**"
— *Booklist,* American Library Association

"**Highly recommended for the young adult audience. Readers will delight in the accessible, energetic, tell-all style; teachers, librarians, and parents will welcome the clever format [and] intelligent and informative text. It should prove especially useful in motivating 'reluctant' readers or literate nonreaders.**"
— *MultiCultural Review*

"**Written in a friendly, almost chatty tone, the profiles offer quick, objective information. While coverage of current figures makes *Biography Today* a useful reference tool, an appealing format and wide scope make it a fun resource to browse.**" — *School Library Journal*

"**The best source for current information at a level kids can understand.**"
— Kelly Bryant, School Librarian, Carlton, OR

"**Easy for kids to read. We love it! Don't want to be without it.**"
— Lynn McWhirter, School Librarian, Rockford, IL

ONE-YEAR SUBSCRIPTION
- 3 softcover issues, 6" x 9"
- Published in January, April, and September
- 1-year subscription, $60
- 150 pages per issue
- 10 profiles per issue
- Contact sources for additional information
- Cumulative Names Index

HARDBOUND ANNUAL CUMULATION
- Sturdy 6" x 9" hardbound volume
- Published in December
- $62 per volume
- 450 pages per volume
- 30 profiles — includes all profiles found in softcover issues for that calendar year
- Cumulative General Index

SUBSCRIPTION AND CUMULATION COMBINATION
- $99 for 3 softcover issues plus the hardbound volume

For Cumulative General, Places of Birth, and Birthday Indexes, please see www.biographytoday.com.

Biography Today

Subject Series

For ages 9 and above

Expands and complements the General Series and targets specific subject areas ...

Our readers asked for it! They wanted more biographies, and the *Biography Today* **Subject Series** is our response to that demand. Now your readers can choose their special areas of interest and go on to read about their favorites in those fields. Priced at just $39 per volume, the following specific volumes are included in the *Biography Today* **Subject Series**:

- **Authors**
- **Business Leaders**
- **Performing Artists**
- **Scientists & Inventors**
- **Sports**

FEATURES AND FORMAT

- Sturdy 6" x 9" hardbound volumes
- Individual volumes, $39 each
- 200 pages per volume
- 10 profiles per volume — targets individuals within a specific subject area
- Contact sources for additional information
- Cumulative General Index

For Cumulative General, Places of Birth, and Birthday Indexes, please see www.biographytoday.com.

NOTE: There is *no duplication of entries* between the **General Series** of *Biography Today* and the **Subject Series**.

AUTHORS

"A useful tool for children's assignment needs." — *School Library Journal*

"The prose is workmanlike: report writers will find enough detail to begin sound investigations, and browsers are likely to find someone of interest." — *School Library Journal*

SCIENTISTS & INVENTORS

"The articles are readable, attractively laid out, and touch on important points that will suit assignment needs. Browsers will note the clear writing and interesting details." — *School Library Journal*

"The book is excellent for demonstrating that scientists are real people with widely diverse backgrounds and personal interests. The biographies are fascinating to read." — *The Science Teacher*

SPORTS

"This series should become a standard resource in libraries that serve intermediate students." — *School Library Journal*